EASY UPGRADES>
BATHROOMS

FROM THE EDITORS OF  **This Old House**

CONTENTS

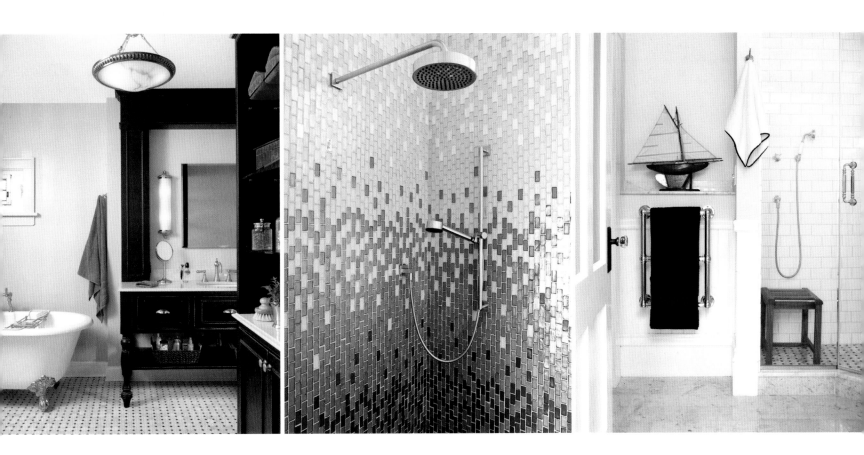

©2010 by Time Home Entertainment Inc.
135 West 50th Street
New York, NY 10020

ISBN-13: 978-0-8487-3394-0
ISBN-10: 0-8487-3394-0
Library of Congress Control Number:
2009941793

Printed in the United States of America
First Printing 2010

Oxmoor House
VP, Publishing Director: **Jim Childs**
Editorial Director: **Susan Payne Dobbs**
Brand Manager: **Fonda Hitchcock**
Managing Editor: **Laurie Herr**

This Old House Ventures Inc.
President: **John L. Brown**
Editor, This Old House: **Scott Omelianuk**
Publisher: **Charles R. Kammerer**

This Old House
Easy Upgrades: Bathrooms
Project Editor: **Laura Goldstein**
Art Director: **Hylah Hill**
Photo Editor: **Denise Sfraga**
Associate Photo Editor: **Allison Chin**
Design Director: **Amy Rosenfeld**
Deputy Editor: **Kathryn Keller**
Design Editor: **Colette Scanlon**
Editorial Operations Director:
Carolyn Blackmar
Editorial Production Manager:
Yoshiko Taniguchi-Canada
Copy Editor: **Jennifer DeMeritt**
Proofreader: **Timothy E. Pitt**
Indexer: **Marjorie Joy**
Prepress Coordinator: **Al Rufino**
Design and Prepress Manager:
Ann-Michelle Gallero
Book Production Manager:
Susan Chodakiewicz

To order additional publications,
call 1-800-765-6400 or 1-800-491-0551.

For more books to enrich your life, visit
oxmoorhouse.com

To subscribe to This Old House, go to
thisoldhouse.com/customerservice
or call 800-898-7237.

For more exciting home and garden ideas, visit **myhomeideas.com**

Front cover photograph: Alise O'Brien; styling by Teanne Chartrau
Back cover photographs (left to right): John Coolidge; Stephen Karlisch; David Prince

THE PERFECT BATH

FOR MORE THAN 30 YEARS, This Old House has been America's top remodeling resource. In that time, we've renovated dozens of bathrooms with the TV cameras running and featured hundreds more in *This Old House* magazine and on thisoldhouse.com. All that experience has taught us plenty about what works and what doesn't, where you should splurge and where you can save—and in *Easy Upgrades,* we're pleased to share that knowledge with you.

Most people's complaints about their bathrooms are similar: outmoded fixtures, outdated design, not enough storage, a layout that doesn't work. On the pages that follow, you'll see how dozens of real-world homeowners solved these common problems to create bathrooms that are long on comfort and brimming with style.

To figure out what kind of space is right for you, start by flipping through the **"Before and After"** case studies and the pages of bathroom **"Idea Files."** In them you'll find inspiration for projects of every type, from a shared bath for the whole gang to a private master retreat to a pocket-size powder room. Next, look at our sample **floor plans** for examples of creative ways to configure space for maximum ease and functionality. Then begin to put it together, with the fixtures,

galleries

Pages filled with great ideas and inspiration

pro advice

Expert tips for getting the bath you want

callouts

Design details you can adapt for any project, no matter how big or small

floor plans

Creative layouts and solutions to common space-planning problems

easy upgrades

Simple ways to get high-end looks at a price you can afford

---

fittings, materials, and finishes that are right for your style and budget.

Throughout this book, you'll see **callouts** highlighting special design details and boxes featuring **advice from *This Old House* pros** on how you can re-create the looks you like in your own home. You'll also find two additional categories of information: **"Easy Upgrades"** are great ideas you can adapt for any project, whether you're taking a room down to the studs or simply making cosmetic changes, while **"Smart Saves"** are expert strategies for cutting costs without cutting corners.

We know remodeling a bath can be stressful. There are more choices than ever

before, and new technologies, while adding comfort, often require more in the way of advance planning and complex construction. Then there's the mess and, of course, the expense—both of which can keep you up at night. After years of helping people improve their spaces, we're realistic enough to acknowledge that there will always be unanticipated hiccups along the way. But if you plan carefully, keep a close eye on your priorities, and invest in the highest quality materials your budget will bear, you'll end up with a space that delivers the pleasure you want and the performance today's families demand. In short, the perfect bath—the one that's right for you.

MAKING BATH TIME FUN doesn't have to be complicated or cost a lot of money. Bright colors, cheerful patterns, and convenient storage turn a basic bath into a space that serves kids and parents alike.

CHAPTER 1>

THE ALL-IN-THE-FAMILY BATH

If money were no object, every member of the family would have his or her own private bath. In the real world, it doesn't work that way. For most households, the bathroom has to serve multiple users—often with competing needs and schedules—and do it at the same time, without sacrificing comfort, style, or functionality. Luckily, as you'll see on the following pages, there are plenty of strategies for designing a bath that pleases every generation, from the youngest members of the household to the oldest.

before +afters

1_ **Shared Bath**

2_ **Bath-and-a-Half**

3_ **Kid-Friendly Bath**

4_ **Barrier-Free Bath**

Open shelving enlivens the facade of a built-in and lets you display favorite items.

before

SHARED BATH

PROBLEM> **The upstairs bath was dark, dated, and cramped.**
SOLUTION> **Turn an unused bedroom into a spacious bath for parents and children.**

BEFORE THE DAYS OF MASTER SUITES with private dressing and washing areas, most old houses had just one lone—and typically tiny—bathroom, used by everyone on the main sleeping floor. So it was with this house, where a small, dim bath served not only the parents but also their young son and their soon-to-be-born baby.

The couple dreamed of a new bath that would be both luxurious and practical, an efficient bathing and grooming space for their growing family. The solution lay in converting an unused bedroom adjacent to the original bath into a new, larger space, claiming the extra square footage for a built-in tub, a separate walk-in shower, a two-sink vanity table, and a wall of built-in storage. The original bathroom has become a dressing area connected to the master bedroom, creating the feel of a private master suite. A second entry off the common hall keeps the bath accessible to the kids.

A vintage-style cabinet with iron strap hinges, a marble-topped vanity table, and board-and-batten wainscoting suit the 1905 house, while eco-friendly materials like recycled glass tile and low-VOC paint give it a modern spin. The result: a beautiful yet functional space for the whole family to enjoy.

after

Transformed, the guest room now serves as a family bath, with built-in storage, double sinks, and a separate tub and shower.

A separate shower saves time: While one parent showers, the other can bathe the kids. →

the plan

Turn an extra bedroom into a bright, comfortable bath for a growing family

1 **CONVERT A BEDROOM.** Taking over an unused bedroom next to the existing bath allowed for a 6-foot tub, walk-in shower, and twin sinks. A dressing area links the new bath to the master bedroom.

2 **EXTEND PLUMBING.** The new bath's location, next to the old one and above the kitchen, made it easier to extend water and waste lines.

3 **MAXIMIZE LIGHT.** A window in the shower, light-reflecting glass tile, and a sunny paint color amp up the brightness.

dressing room

4 **BUILD IN STORAGE.** A custom floor-to-ceiling cabinet holds toiletries, towels, and a pullout laundry hamper.

THE WIDE MARBLE TUB SURROUND provides a comfortable perch for the parents while they bathe their young kids, plus plenty of surface area for keeping toys and towels close at hand.

SMART SAVE

Adding windows not only makes a space more pleasant, it reduces the need for artificial lighting and saves money in the long run.

the **details** Luxury and efficiency combine in a space that has built-in kid conveniences plus spa-like amenities for the grown-ups

↓**RECYCLED GLASS TILE** in two different sizes and colors lines the shower and the built-in niche that holds soap and shampoo.

↓**THE OAK VANITY** with marble top, though new, nods to the fine craftsmanship of the early 1900s, when the house was built.

←**A CUSTOM STORAGE UNIT** is fitted with pullout bins for dirty laundry, open cubbies for towels, cabinets for hiding extra TP, and drawers for grooming supplies as well as stickers—given to the toddler as toilet-training rewards.

SMART SAVE

Using domestic materials, like this floor slate mined in the U.S. instead of shipped from abroad, keeps construction costs down.

Customizing built-ins

TIPS FROM
COLETTE SCANLON,
TOH DESIGN
EDITOR

Nothing puts your square footage to better use than a built-in. Whether it's a floor-to-ceiling storage cabinet like the one in this bathroom, or a narrow shelving unit recessed between wall studs, built-ins let you squeeze every available inch from your floor plan. Here are some ways to plan built-ins for maximum style and functionality.

1 Treat them like furniture. To give built-in cabinets and wardrobes a furniture look, don't run the units all the way up to the ceiling; top them with crown molding that matches what's elsewhere in the house, and give the pieces feet or legs, which also help to lighten the look.

2 Take advantage of found space. The beauty of built-ins is that they can be custom crafted for those odd nooks and crannies where a standard piece might not fit, such as between wall studs or in plumbing chases.

3 Build out, too. Built-ins that create an alcove for freestanding furniture can call attention to a favorite piece. Built-in shelving or cabinets flanking an antique vanity table, for instance, could provide close-at-hand storage for towels and toiletries, eliminating the need for a medicine cabinet over the sink.

BATH-AND-A-HALF

PROBLEM> **The family's only bathtub was in the parents' master suite.**
SOLUTION> **Carve the master bath into two rooms so that the kids can access the tub.**

REPLACING BATHTUBS WITH SHOWER STALLS is one way to free up bathroom space in an old house. But it can also spell a long wait for family members who want to have a leisurely soak in the one remaining tub. The challenge for these homeowners, who opted for stall showers throughout the house, was finding a way to give their athletic children access to the new jetted spa tub they planned to install in their master suite addition while preserving a private cleanup area for themselves.

The game plan: Divide the bathroom in two, with the tub and shower in one room and a sink and the toilet in an adjoining half bath. Such a split would mean no kids hammering on the door or holding the bathroom hostage in the evening while the parents want to get ready for bed.

Appointed with wainscoting and vintage-look fixtures, the two parts of the bathroom are united by a turn-of-the-century English style that complements the rest of the 1917 Tudor. The result is one split decision where everybody wins.

A simple ledge of molding allows for an ever-changing art display. →

→ **THE MARBLE-TOPPED TUB SURROUND** has a clipped corner to keep people from nicking their shins on the way to the shower or sink.

the plan

Create separate tub and toilet rooms to give the whole family access to the bath

1 ADD ACCESSIBLE STORAGE. A generous linen closet just outside the tub room door can be easily reached on the way to either part of the bath.

2 CREATE AN ADJOINING HALF BATH. Locating the toilet and a second sink in a separate room allows members of the family to use different parts of the master bath at the same time without sacrificing privacy.

3 DESIGNATE A TUB/ SHOWER ROOM. The 6-foot-long tub at the center of the new master bath shares the main room with a 3-by-6-foot steam shower and a single sink.

the details White wainscoting and an interior window keep the space airy and bright while also giving it period authenticity

← **A LEADED-GLASS WINDOW** filters light from the bath into a stairwell. White-painted beadboard wainscoting adds to the turn-of-the-century look.

SMART SAVE

For interior applications like this one, where energy efficiency isn't an issue, an old accent window from the salvage yard is a great choice—typically cheaper than a reproduction and longer on character.

Creative ways to use wainscot

TIPS FROM

COLETTE SCANLON, TOH DESIGN EDITOR

Wainscot isn't just traditional, it's also practical, especially in high-traffic areas like a family bath. It can warm up a room filled with cold porcelain fixtures, ceramic floors, and tiled tub enclosures. In this house, the same beadboard wainscoting treatment unites the tub and toilet rooms and ties them in with the rest of the home's architecture. Here are some other ways to use wainscot wisely.

1 **Vary the height.** Historically, wainscoting extended about one-third of the way up the wall, to protect against damage from chair backs. In a bathroom, there's no fixed formula for wainscot height. In fact, you can use it to compensate for other layout issues. In a low-ceilinged space, for instance, low wainscot will make the room appear taller. Higher-than-normal wainscot tends to give a space a more formal look.

2 **Consider different materials.** Beadboard is the classic choice, but it's not the only (or even the best) option in the bath, where moisture can be an issue. Specially treated medium-density fiberboard, solid surfacing, and cellular PVC look like wood and help protect the drywall or plaster underneath from water damage. A pricier option is ceramic "beadboard," which combines a classic look with the durability and water-resistance of tile.

A bumped-out wall that hides plumbing can → double as a handy shelf.

→ **THE TOILET AND A SINK** are in a separate half bath, so they're accessible when the tub or shower is occupied. The two sinks—pedestal here, console in the tub room—are complementary but not matching.

Windows at either end of the unfinished attic were reserved for future bedrooms, which meant the new interior bath would have to manage without natural light.

before

KID-FRIENDLY BATH

PROBLEM> **The daughter's new attic bath lacked windows.**
SOLUTION> **Lighten and brighten with a playful paint job and crisp white walls.**

OLD-HOUSE BATHROOMS are seldom designed with kids in mind. The tub's too deep, the sink's too high, and there's never enough storage for bath toys. So the owners of this 1885 house decided to build their young daughter a bath that would be just her size. Problem was, they would have to carve the new space out of the middle of the unfinished attic, reserving windows at either end for bedrooms they planned to add later.

Though it gets no natural light, the 75-square-foot space is anything but dark and dreary. Bold paint colors, big mirrors, and lots of white more than compensate for the lack of windows. The room is long on vintage charm, too. A corner kitchen sink and a 4-foot pedestal tub, both salvaged from elsewhere in the house, nail the period look. Now, with such bright and cheerful surroundings, bath time is fun for parents and child alike.

after

Even without windows, the new bath feels luminous because of paint-striped walls, multicolored cubbies, white wainscot and floor tile, and semigloss ceiling paint.

EASY UPGRADE

It's simple to dress up your wall with painted stripes. All you need is a pencil, ruler, and level. Outline the stripes in pencil, then use a small velour-covered roller to fill in with latex paint.

Semigloss enamel paint protects wood in a tub area because it sheds water. →

→WALL-HUNG MIRRORS that look like big bubbles tilt down for a child's-eye view, and the sink's drainboard serves as an easy-to-clean counter.

↑ Who says you need a bath sink? This former kitchen sink works like a charm.

the plan

Carve a pint-size bath out of the center of an unfinished attic

1 **MAXIMIZE FLOOR SPACE.** The pocket door eliminates a door swing and eases traffic flow around the sink.

2 **ADD A FOCAL POINT.** A tucked-away toilet is hidden from view until you enter the room, keeping the focus on the painted pedestal tub.

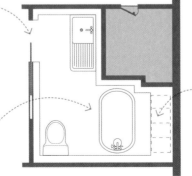

3 **BUILD IN STORAGE.** Cubbies exploit a void behind the 4-foot tub. The colorful storage recesses keep the room open and airy, with toys and towels handy at bath time.

the details

Bright colors, bold patterns, and reflective surfaces make up for a lack of natural light

↓ STORAGE CUBBIES, which repeat the six paint shades of the stripes that ring the room, frame the tub with color and stand in for a linen closet.

SMART SAVE

Open shelving not only adds convenience and style, it's also more budget friendly than closed cabinetry.

→ VINTAGE-LOOK TUB FITTINGS, including a gooseneck faucet and telephone-style hand shower, make it easy to rinse off a soapy kid.

↑ A CHEERFUL BORDER in the hexagonal-tile floor adds impact for a lot less money than an allover pattern.

✳ TOH DESIGN ADVICE

Even if you've got open space behind the wall, avoid making cubbies more than 18 inches deep, or you'll lose track of items.

BARRIER-FREE BATH

PROBLEM: The existing kids' bath was okay for the son but too small for a daughter who used a wheelchair.
SOLUTION: Open up the floor plan, and create a shared bath that meets the needs of both children.

DESIGNING A BATH FOR KIDS can be tricky—you want to make the space fun and easy for them to use now, but timeless enough to suit them as they get older. In the case of this bath, there was an added challenge: One of the children used a wheelchair, which meant the room had to be planned with the different needs of both children in mind.

The result offers ample proof that a universally accessible bath can also be beautiful. The centerpiece of the space is a luminous, curved wall covered in glass tile in shades of purple, gold, and green. On one side is a double-sink vanity, with one basin at conventional height for the son and a lower sink for the daughter, both equipped with touchless faucets. On the other side of the wall is a large wheel-in shower stall with plenty of light, thanks to a casement window high on the wall.

Though the daughter, a young teen, helped choose the colors and finishes, the space is neutral enough for her brother and sophisticated enough for the adults who often use it as a guest bath, since it's the one closest to the home's public areas. Now bright, open, and easy to navigate, the bathroom is not just universally accessible, it's universally appealing, too.

The new bath is bright, cheerful, and functional, with an open layout and a wheel-in shower with adjustable fixtures.

Electronic faucets are easy to operate and also fun for kids to use.
↓

→ A WALL-TO-WALL MIRROR, a quartz counterop flecked with bits of seashells, and a light-colored porcelain tile floor make the space look big and bright.

the plan

Open the space, update the finishes, and build in accessibility features

1   OPEN UP FLOOR SPACE. Taking out the tub and stealing a few feet from an adjacent laundry room made space for a generous shower stall.

2   ADD DOUBLE VANITIES. Set at different heights, one sink is dropped into the vanity, and the other is wall mounted to fit a wheelchair underneath.

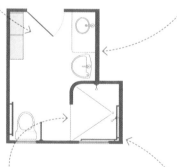

3   BUILD A WHEEL-IN SHOWER. The shower, set off behind a curved glass wall, has no curb to block access and room for a wheelchair to turn around.

4   CUSTOMIZE THE DETAILS. Adjustable shower fittings meet the needs of different users, as do wall niches set at different heights.

A wall-mounted vanity shelf leaves plenty of room for a wheelchair to slide in underneath. ↓

＊ TOH DESIGN ADVICE
Even if you don't need them now, build in smart features that let you age in place—such as a wider doorway, seating in the shower, and blocking behind walls so that you can easily add grab bars later.

AGING GRACEFULLY

FIXTURES AND FITTINGS for an adaptable bath come in all sorts of styles, as this more traditional interpretation shows. Built for a mother-in-law who uses a walker and occasionally a wheelchair, the ground-floor bath also functions as a powder room for guests.

The accessibility features are so well integrated that you may not be able to spot them all. The floor tiles, for instance, were chosen for their small size, which offers greater traction for wheelchair tires and makes them less slippery underfoot than larger ones. The entire bathroom, in fact, functions as a roll-in shower stall, with a vinyl membrane covering the floor and running 12 inches up the wall for maximum water protection.

↓ THE VITREOUS CHINA SINK, though old-fashioned in style, is a wall-mount model, so it can be hung high enough to allow a wheelchair to glide under. A 6-foot-tall recessed medicine cabinet provides plenty of storage that can be easily reached.

↑ GRAB BARS in the shower are aligned with a band of accent tile so that they look like an integral part of the design and not an afterthought. The shower controls are easy-to-turn lever handles mounted 33 inches above the floor, the ideal height for wheelchair users. A plastic Chippendale-inspired outdoor chair adds comfort and safety in traditional style.

← A TALLER TOILET meets ADA guidelines that specify a seat 17 to 19 inches high—2 inches more than standard—to make it more comfortable for people who have difficulty bending.

← A SLIDING POCKET DOOR replaces a standard hinged door. It's easy to pull open and closed, and the absence of a door swing keeps floor space clear.

A MASTER BATH is all about individual expression, whether that comes in the form of high-end materials or, as here, a mahogany dresser discovered at the Salvation Army.

CHAPTER 2

THE MASTER BATH

We all dream about having a master bath, a personal sanctuary where we can cast off the stresses of the day and indulge our senses with a luxurious soak or a relaxing steam shower. Well, the qualities that make a successful master bath—privacy, warmth, light, convenience—come not from the biggest spaces or the most expensive fixtures and finishes (though we've got plenty of eye-popping examples in these pages), but from thoughtful design that meets the needs of the user. And that's within reach of any budget.

before + afters

Fixed transom windows set high above the tub let in light without compromising privacy.

UP-TO-DATE TRADITIONAL

PROBLEM> The existing bath was too small for a fully kitted-out master.
SOLUTION> Commandeer an extra bedroom to make space for modern conveniences.

ADDING A BATHROOM to a period house can be tricky. You don't want to make it too contemporary, but you want to include every modern convenience, like a steam shower and soaking tub. This bath, in a Federal-style house built in the 1920s, has it all: the shower and tub, plus lots of storage and a dressing closet—and a look that respects tradition while adapting it for today's needs.

To get their dream master bath, the homeowners converted an extra bedroom at the back of the house rather than expand their existing small bathroom. Period influences are evident in the wainscot paneling, faux-ebony baseboards, and pedestal soaking tub. But the travertine floor, black-framed doors and windows, and granite countertops give it a contemporary edge.

Pale yellow walls and French doors leading to the bedroom make the space "light, bright, and elegant," say the homeowners, who wanted to stay away from the all-white look typical of many early-20th-century bathrooms. And even though the bath is all new, it fits right in with the rest of the house.

after

The new bath, in a former bedroom, is finished with details that tie it in with the rest of the 1920s-era house: recessed-panel wainscot, black-painted baseboards, and fixed transom windows. Black-framed doors and windows and a marble-tile floor lend some contemporary touches.

→ **WOOD-FRAMED MEDICINE CABINETS** are recessed into the wall and finished with contemporary-style brushed-pewter pulls. The sconces are period reproductions.

↑ The furniturelike double vanity is actually a kitchen island the owners fell in love with at the showroom.

the *plan*

Carve out a new master bathroom, with all the bells and whistles

1 **EXPAND THE SPACE.** A 240-square-foot bumpout off the master bath created a new master bedroom, connected by French doors.

2 **ADD CLOSETS.** The old bedroom closet was enlarged to create a dressing closet and a linen closet, both off the bath.

to master bedroom

dressing closet

3 **PUT IN A DOUBLE VANITY.** The 5½-foot-long console holds his-and-hers sinks, and has plenty of storage and an ample granite deck.

4 **BUILD IN PRIVACY.** A separate WC and shower stall make the shared space easier to use.

the details

Fixtures and finishes work together to tweak a traditional style

→ **FRENCH DOORS** with horizontally divided lights lead to the master bedroom; they are painted black to match the baseboards and window trim. Opaque glass provides privacy while letting in natural light.

↓ **THE DOUBLE VANITY,** made of cherry and topped with granite, provides plenty of deck space on top; drawers and an open shelf offer ample storage below.

Glass knobs look equally at home on traditional and modern door styles.

→ **THE TRAVERTINE FLOOR** gets added visual interest from the different-size field tiles on either side of a 3-inch-wide mosaic border. Outside the border are 12-inch squares; inside, the tiles were trimmed 3 inches and laid in a running-bond brick pattern.

EASY UPGRADE

An inset strip of a different material can elevate the look of even the plainest floor tile. Plus, it allows you to use a smaller amount of a more expensive material for maximum visual effect.

↑ **THE TUB FILLER** has a vintage look, with a sleek swan-neck faucet, cross handles with porcelain insets, and a handheld spray, all in a satin nickel finish appropriate to the period.

ADDED-ON BATH

PROBLEM> **The family was outgrowing their house, but they didn't want to move.**
SOLUTION> **Build an addition and get the traditional-style master bath of their dreams.**

IT'S HARD TO LEAVE A PLACE you've grown to love. So when it came time to look for a bigger house to accommodate their growing family, these homeowners found one right in their own backyard. Literally. An addition on the back of the house would give them all the space they needed for the kids, and it would allow them to build a luxurious master suite for themselves.

Their new master bath is a marriage of traditional styling with modern amenities. From the pair of polished-nickel console sinks to the marble basket-weave-tile floors to the old-fashioned pedestal soaking tub, every element is rooted in old-world elegance. Though the statement is luxury to the max, it's whispered rather than shouted, with muted colors, subtle details, and lots of open floor space.

From the tub, it's a short pad in bare feet to the coffeemaker and beverage refrigerator just outside the bathroom door, then back across to the adjacent sitting area. With a setup like that, who'd ever want to leave?

after

Traditional materials, like those in the Calacatta-marble-topped console sinks, wood-framed medicine cabinets, basket-weave floors, and subway-tile walls, give the new addition a timeless look.

A PEDESTAL TUB takes center stage. All the bath fittings, including the train-style towel rack, are polished nickel.

the plan

Create a spa-like and serene master bath in a newly constructed addition

1 **ESTABLISH A FOCAL POINT.** The tub anchors the large space and offers scenic views of an old barn through the large windows above.

2 **BUILD IN PRIVACY.** The WC is in its own room to one side of the tub, with a door that closes.

3 **ADD AMENITIES.** A beverage center right outside the bathroom door has a small bar sink, refrigerator, and coffeemaker. A door to the left of the sinks leads to an adjacent sitting area.

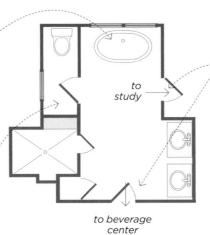

to study

to beverage center

the details

Subtle colors, traditional fixtures, and plenty of light and open space add up to a soothing atmosphere

→ **PORCELAIN LEVERS**, exposed risers, and Victorian "rose" rainheads give the shower a true vintage style.

↓ **A SOFFIT** over the tub alcove visually lowers the ceiling and helps create a sense of intimacy. Recessed lights illuminate the tub for nighttime bathing.

← **SUBWAY TILE** set in a running-bond pattern lines the shower, which has two sets of controls and a built-in bench.

EASY UPGRADE

If you like the vintage look of exposed plumbing, old-style hand showers, mounted on vertical bars, are simple to retrofit.

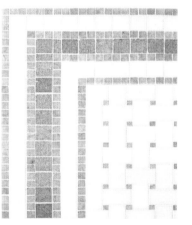

← **TINY MOSAIC** tiles form a border that complements the basket-weave floor and helps tie the large space together. The pattern even extends into the shower stall.

TOH DESIGN ADVICE

Old-fashioned cast-iron tubs are beautiful but heavy, especially when fully loaded with bathers and water. Be sure your floor supports can withstand the weight.

The bedroom of a rental unit, carved out of the house's second floor in the 1950s, occupied the space that would become the new master bath and dressing area.

before

ACROSS-THE-HALL BATH

PROBLEM> **The rowhouse had no bathroom on the sleeping floor.**
SOLUTION> **Take over a bedroom for a master bath, and make it accessible to the kids, too.**

GENERALLY, IT'S GOOD to avoid stairs in the black of night. But what do you do if the only bathroom in the house is down a flight of 13 steps—and through the dining room, kitchen, and a hallway?

The existing master bedroom in this 1853 rowhouse was the only room on the second floor, thanks to a rental apartment that had been carved out in the 1950s. The owners longed for a master bath within shuffling distance of their bedroom. So, as part of their long-held plan to restore the building's single-family configuration, they reclaimed the rental unit and converted it into a vintage-look master bathroom and dressing area. As a bonus, the couple's daughter got spacious digs as well.

While they wanted the new bath to feel right for the 19th-century home, they also wanted 21st-century amenities, like a glass-walled steam shower. The re-design entailed a few compromises—having to cross the hall to get from bedroom to bath, for one—but the couple has no complaints. And it sure beats trekking downstairs in the middle of the night.

after

Vintage-style finishes, like beadboard paneling and white subway tile, help the new room look at home in the 19th-century house. A lean-legged console sink and a wood-framed medicine cabinet add to the room's old-fashioned appearance.

An interior window brings natural light into an otherwise windowless space.

→ **A PEDESTAL SINK** in the toilet room creates the illusion of his-and-hers baths. Frosted-glass panes in the door allow light while preserving privacy.

the plan

Add a master bath where none existed, and make it accessible to both upstairs bedrooms

1 **ANNEX A BEDROOM.** The combined bath and dressing area are in the bedroom of the former rental unit.

2 **SPLIT THE BATH.** To allow for multiple users at once, the 35-square-foot main room holds the shower and a sink. A second sink was added to the 25-square-foot toilet room.

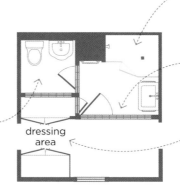

dressing area

3 **BUMP OUT A WALL.** Expanding 15 inches into the adjacent bedroom made room for an oversize shower and lots of storage.

4 **ADD WINDOWS.** Clerestory windows and doors with frosted-glass panels bring natural light into the bath.

5 **CREATE A DRESSING AREA.** An interior wall sections off the dressing area from the bath. Entries at either end create an easy flow between the master bedroom, the bathroom, and the child's room at the opposite end of the hall.

the details

19th-century-appropriate materials disguise a space filled with modern amenities

↓ **FRAMELESS GLASS DOORS** with square hinges create a sleek shower enclosure.

← **BEADBOARD PANELING** lends an antique look to the newly built bath, while radiant heat under the floor tile keeps the room toasty.

EASY UPGRADE

A heated towel rack adds warmth and style to any bath, and helps chase the chill from the room.

Built-in wardrobes hold more than a closet and add character. ←

→ **RETRO BLACK-DOT TILE** on the shower floor mixes with marble mosaic and more modern 12-by-12-inch squares of Carrara marble.

↑ **A WIDE-PLANK FLOOR** made from reclaimed white-oak barn wood helps give the new dressing area its old-house feel.

The island's curves and angles give it a sculptural look. The tub surround, vanity sides, and columns are wrapped in walnut beadboard. The porcelain vessel sink, an update on a washbasin, tops the vanity, which slants inward—a stylish way to create foot room.

ISLAND BATH

PROBLEM> An open-plan bath needed visual interest.
SOLUTION> Divide the space with a central island that looks like a piece of sculpture.

MOST PEOPLE WALK THROUGH a bathroom showroom ogling the high-end sinks, luxurious steam showers, and gleaming chrome faucets. But what struck the owner of this bath as she was shopping for fixtures were the ceiling-hung mirrors that partitioned off different room vignettes. "I couldn't get them out of my mind," she says.

Newlyweds, she and her husband were planning a master-suite addition with a big, open bath that would have a contemporary feel. But they didn't want a room ringed with fixtures. When they told their designer about the showroom mirrors, he came up with an innovative plan for the 300-square-foot space: a central island with a floor-to-ceiling "partition" made up of two columns with a mirror hung in between. The vanity is on one side, a spa tub on the other, dividing the unit—and the entire room—into separate bathing and grooming areas.

To tie the bath to the rest of the 1880s farmhouse, the same yellow pine floors and beadboard paneling carry over into the new space, where they lend warmth to contemporary glass, stone, and steel. Stone-look ceramic tile complements the wood tones, and big windows flood the room with natural light.

A tilt-open transom window in the shower lets steam escape. ↓

39

the plan

Create a dramatic centerpiece and divide the master bathroom into separate zones for grooming and soaking

1 DIVIDE THE SPACE. A central, two-sided island unites the tub and vanity as it breaks up open space.

walk-in closet

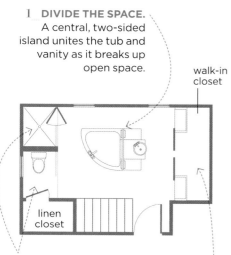

linen closet

2 SEPARATE THE TOILET AND SHOWER. A glassed-in shower and partially enclosed toilet alcove occupy the wall opposite the tub.

3 ADD CLOSETS. Built-in shelves and pullout bins create his-and-hers dressers. Sliding doors lead to a generous walk-in closet, and a linen closet tucks in under the stairs.

→ **THE TWO-WAY VANITY MIRROR is** reflective above the sink but transparent on the tub side, where you enter the room.

↑ Tight-grained mahogany is naturally resistant to moisture.

the details

Warm woods mix with modern materials to create an eclectic yet serene space

→ **ITALIAN CERAMIC TILE** lining the shower stall is made to look like granite. Stainless-steel corner shelves hold soap and shampoo.

↓ **THE WEDGE-SHAPED SPA TUB** has two straight sides that each measure 48 inches long. The couple chose the configuration for its visual interest.

→ **THE GRANITE VANITY COUNTERTOP** extends under the hanging mirror and cantilevers over the edge of the tub, providing a handy perch for bath toiletries.

↑ **WALNUT SLIDING DOORS** on the closet intentionally evoke a barn door as a way to bring a farm feeling into the new bathroom.

SMART SAVE

Pullout bins and open shelves maximize storage space, convenience, and cost when compared with fully enclosed cabinetry.

Recessing the cabinets in the side wall keeps the lines of the mirror clean and unbroken.

PERFECT PAIRING

PROBLEM> **The architect's plan called for separate baths for husband and wife.** SOLUTION> **Convert "her" bath into "theirs," and add plenty of shared amenities.**

THE FRAMING HAD JUST GONE UP on the stone-and-shingle house when a newly married couple fell in love with the architect's vision and bought the place—then they set about customizing the interior to their liking. They were not only able to select their own finishes, but also to alter the plan for the master bath. The architect had designed two separate baths flanking the master bedroom, a growing trend for master suites today. But the new owners decided they'd prefer one shared master bath and a bedroom sitting area instead.

So "her" bath became "theirs," and "his" became the sitting room at the entry to the master suite. In keeping with the overall aesthetic of the house, the bathroom combines classic architectural details, such as a vaulted cove ceiling, wainscoted walls, and arched moldings, with luxurious materials, like Brazilian cherry and Crema Marfil marble. To bring some color and a sense of intimacy to the room, the couple chose sky-blue and beige patterned wallpaper to cover the top half of the walls.

For the homeowners, the room encapsulates everything they love about the house. Says the wife, "It's traditional and a bit formal, but not too much so."

after

The handsome double vanity is made from natural cherry and topped with the same beige marble that lines the walls and floor. Husband and wife have dedicated storage in medicine cabinets on either side of the arched mirror.

AN ARCHED MOLDING DETAIL, one of several in the room, echoes the cove ceiling and ties together the WC and shower doors.

Adding color to the upper half of the wall helps create a sense of intimacy. →

the plan

Create a well-appointed bath for him and her with plenty of natural light and spa-like luxuries

1 KEEP IT LIGHT.
Three windows over the tub, plus one in the toilet room, bring in plenty of natural light. Sky-blue paint on the vaulted cove ceiling enhances the airy effect.

2 DOUBLE UP ON SINKS.
"Her" proposed space became a shared master bath with the addition of a second sink at one end of the 8½-by-22-foot room. The skirted tub in the center anchors the space, and the WC and shower occupy the opposite wall.

3 LOAD UP ON AMENITIES.
A multispray steam shower, a jetted spa tub, radiant floor heating, a towel warmer, and stereo speakers built into the walls create a relaxing, luxurious environment.

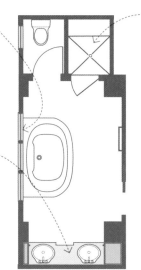

Hints of color and pattern relax the formal setting, while architectural elements unite disparate materials

↑**THE MARBLE-LINED** steam shower is equipped with a built-in bench and multiple showerheads and body sprays. Contrasting tile lines the shallow niche for soap and shampoo.

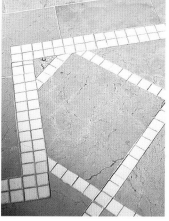

↑**THE VAULTED COVE CEILING, an** architectural motif found elsewhere in the house, is painted blue to echo the wallpaper and mimic the sky.

EASY UPGRADE

A touch of color on the ceiling can warm things up and give a space a more finished look.

↑**A PATTERN** of 1¼-inch white marble tiles surrounding 12-inch beige marble tiles is laid like a rug, following the shape of the room and marking out the central area. The mosaic border is echoed in the wall tile that rings the room.

*TOH DESIGN ADVICE

Creating a pattern on the floor with contrasting colors and materials helps to visually organize a large room.

before

An all-beige color scheme and clunky built-ins made the bath cramped and uninteresting.

MASCULINE MASTER

PROBLEM> The old bath was plain and cramped, and the shower leaked into the living room.
SOLUTION> Remove the bulky built-ins, and create an elegant, functional space with masculine details.

THE HOMEOWNER'S PLAN was to live with the old, boring bath while he redid the kitchen—until the shower started leaking into his living room. Then, fixing the bath quickly shot to the top of the priority list for the circa-1910 house. The first order of business: getting rid of the bulky built-ins, dated tilework, and cramped layout. "I wanted to throw three grenades in there and blow the whole thing up," he says. "It wasn't visually interesting, and it didn't feel fun."

Inspired by a small piece of antique stained glass the owner found while traveling in London, the design fell into place easily. Shrinking the large (and privacy-robbing) window over the tub gave the decorative glass a home and allowed for a more open configuration, even with the addition of a deep clawfoot soaking tub and large glassed-in shower stall. Leaving the plumbing lines in their existing locations saved some cash for high-end amenities, like an alabaster-shaded light fixture and custom cabinetry with just the right amount of storage. The new bath has the look of an English gentleman's space that is stately but simple—and, of course, watertight.

after

The new bath is simple and elegant, with dark-stained maple cabinetry given a slightly distressed finish to keep it from looking stark. Light-colored Crema Marfil marble countertops and floor tiles provide contrast and add a luxurious touch.

→ **MARBLE SLABS** lining the shower are easy to clean (no grout lines) and easy on the eyes. Floor-to-ceiling glass partitions keep the space feeling open and the large rainhead on display.

EASY UPGRADE
A paint treatment that alternates flat and glossy stripes carries the eye around the room and adds subtle panache in an otherwise tailored space.

Don't underestimate the power of a tiny towel to pack a big visual punch.
↓

the plan

Open the space without moving the plumbing to keep bucks in the budget for luxe amenities

1 **SHRINK THE WINDOW.** The smaller one is more bath-appropriate and frees up wall space for the claw-foot tub while still letting in light.

2 **TURN THE TUB.** Flipping the tub to the wall opposite the shower opens up floor space, and getting rid of the surround allows both tub and shower to be larger.

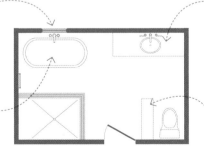

3 **DOWNSIZE THE VANITY.** A single sink with a generous surround has a sleeker look and plenty of storage.

4 **ADD A PARTITION.** A floor-to-ceiling built-in adds architectural interest while providing easy-to-access storage and privacy for the toilet area.

the **details**

Clean lines and handsome appointments create a room with just the right feeling of understated elegance

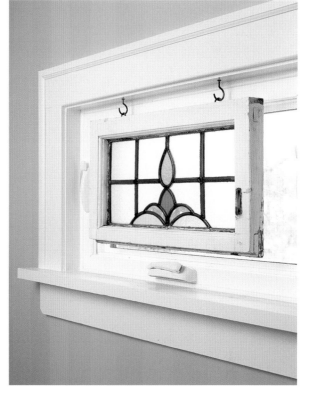

→ **ANTIQUE STAINED GLASS** inspired the bath's European feel. Its gray leading is picked up in the metal finishes.

↑ **A BUILT-IN HUTCH** adds storage and privacy, but the open shelving doesn't compromise the room's spacious feeling.

→ **SATIN NICKEL KNOBS** on the cabinets and cupped bin pulls on the vanity drawers have an appropriate vintage look.

← **WALL SCONCES** with glass diffusers flank the recessed medicine cabinet. They can dim for general soft illumination or provide bright task light for shaving.

← **METAL TUB FEET** show off the detail in the design while adding subtle ornamentation to the room.

49

CHAPTER 3
THE HALF BATH

When it comes to making a style statement, there's no better place to do it than the powder room. Because these two-fixture baths are used most often by guests, they lend themselves to showcase treatment—so deck them out with sculptural sinks, handcrafted fittings, and decorative wall finishes. You don't need much to make a powder room feel special: just one standout fixture or material, as you'll see here. And given its small scale, a powder room is one place where you can always afford a splurge.

A PETITE PEDESTAL SINK keeps a snug 4-by-5-foot space from feeling cramped. Because powder rooms are usually located near the public areas of a house, it makes sense to carry over architectural details from surrounding spaces. Here, the edges of the basin and pedestal base echo the moldings in and around the half bath.

IDEA FILE

Because a half bath doesn't have strict requirements for space, light, and fixtures, it's an ideal place to showcase style without sacrificing functionality

↑HANDCRAFTED CHARACTER All the surfaces in this cozy space have an artisanal look, from the mottled yellow walls to the green-glazed pedestal to the patinated-copper garden urn that serves as a sink. The oil-rubbed bronze faucet is mounted to the mirror, which also acts as the backsplash.

←MISSION UPDATE Leaded-glass details on the cherry vanity doors and mirror lend this room a contemporary Arts and Crafts style. Wall sconces with traditional detailing and a pewter-finish faucet reinforce the look. The ample 4-foot-wide vanity provides plenty of space for guest towels and toiletries.

← STONE STATEMENT

You can do things in a powder room that would be impractical in a larger space. This 2,000-pound slab of Yosemite slate, used here as a vanity top, took eight men to set in place.

↑ FARMHOUSE FRESH Painted panel wainscoting and simple details evoke 19th-century farmhouse style. But the owners wanted their guest bath to convey the idea of an antique house that had been "modernized" in the 1920s, hence the chunky pedestal sink and patterned wallpaper.

Fitting in a half bath

TIPS FROM

COLETTE SCANLON, TOH DESIGN EDITOR

A powder room is a smart addition—by one estimate, it can increase a home's resale value by more than 10 percent. If you're thinking about squeezing one into an existing house, the first challenge is figuring out where to put it. Here are a few ways to carve out a half bath that'll give you your money's worth.

1 **Consider "hidden" spaces.** Look for a space that is close to the main entertaining areas, but avoid plumbing a wall shared with the living or dining room, where you don't want the added noise. Consider tucking it into the recess under a staircase or converting a large first-floor closet.

2 **Follow the line.** To save on costs, stay close to adjacent plumbing so that you can tap into the existing water and drain lines. Adding new lines drives up costs a lot, especially if they're on an outside wall and need insulation.

3 **Account for the door swing.** Ideally, the door should open in, so as not to impede traffic flow at the bath entrance. In really tight spaces the door may have to open out, or you can install a sliding pocket door.

4 **Test-drive the layout.** Always dry-fit fixtures before installing them so that you know exactly how their placement will work. You don't want to find out you can't get around the open door after you've installed the wash basin.

→ **TRADITIONAL WITH A TWIST**

A distressed cherry cabinet with a zinc countertop, curved backsplash, and vessel sink evokes the spirit of an old-fashioned washstand. Over time, the zinc will develop a deep patina.

EASY UPGRADE

For that inspired-by-the-past look, try hanging carriage lanterns instead of more conventional bath sconces.

↑ ECLECTIC Wrapped in wainscoting that reflects the house's Craftsman feel and echoes the paneling in the nearby hallway, this bath is outfitted with a solid oak vanity with a limestone top and backsplash, and a bridge-style faucet with an oil-rubbed bronze finish.

↓ COTTAGE CHARM Beadboard wainscoting, clean-lined fixtures, and soothing colors make a small space comfortable and inviting. For a bit of contrast that doesn't overwhelm, the black-and-white floor gets a boost from a colored border, and the stained-wood mirror and shelf stand out against the light walls.

TOH DESIGN ADVICE

In a small powder room, the ceiling should be no taller than 8 feet, to avoid a vertical tunnel effect. If it's any higher, you may want to paint it a deep color to make the space feel more intimate.

BATH FITTINGS with chrome or porcelain cross handles, and an elaborate swan-neck tub filler with hand shower, provide the finishing touches in a traditional bath.

CHAPTER 4 >
THE VINTAGE-LOOK BATH

These days, it's easier than ever to give an up-to-date bath a period look. Victorian, Craftsman, Art Deco—whatever your style, manufacturers offer suites of fixtures that have all the charm of the originals, plus performance that meets today's demands. Perhaps the most enduring look is the classic turn-of-the-century bath, with its chrome-legged washstands, marble floors, and subway tile walls. With so many products at every price point—not just tubs and toilets but also towel bars, soap dishes, and vanity mirrors—it's simple to add a sprinkling of period flavor to even the smallest bath project.

before
+afters

1_ **Classic Bath**

2_ **Art Deco Bath**

3_ **Victorian Bath**

4_ **Craftsman Bath**

Uplighting bounces light off the walls and ceiling for nice, even illumination.

An open area under the sink visually expands the room (just be sure to account for storage needs).

A misguided bath remodel shouted 1980s. It lacked both practicality and privacy, with the toilet on display between the shower and the partially enclosed tub.

before

CLASSIC BATH

PROBLEM> The master bath had been badly remodeled, and the children's bath was overcrowded. **SOLUTION>** Shuffle rooms to make a bigger, brighter master and more elbow room for the kids.

ALL IT TAKES IS ONE "AHA" MOMENT to make life easier for a whole family. In this case, the homeowners' need to reimagine their space grew out of the realization that their three boys—an 11-year-old and 8-year-old twins—were bumping elbows in the hall bathroom they shared. Just when the parents were drawing up plans to update their master bath, the victim of a botched 1980s-style redo, the project looked as if it would be trumped by their sons' needs.

Then the architect hit on an inspired solution. His plan worked like a slide puzzle, starting with the elimination of a seldom-used sitting room in the master suite. By shifting the master bedroom into that space, he could move the master bath into the former bedroom and slip a new kids' bath in its place.

Now there's peace in the house, plus a master bath that gets great light (thanks to the former bedroom's multiple windows) and has a more user-friendly flow, with separate zones for the toilet, shower, and tub. And the turn-of-the-century home finally got the classic bath it had long deserved.

after

The windowed space that was formerly the master bedroom makes a perfect location for the new marble-topped double console sink and wood-framed, recessed medicine cabinets.

→ **THE VINTAGE-LOOK TUB** with its Edwardian-style faucet has pride of place beneath a large triple window.

the plan

Make space for a larger, more efficient master bathroom and an expanded kids' bath by sacrificing an unused sitting room

1 REASSIGN ROOMS. Part of the old master bathroom went to create a second, smaller kids' bath, while the new master bath took the place of the master bedroom, which slid over into a rarely used sitting-room space. The new bath has separate zones for the toilet, shower, sink, and tub.

2 CONTROL TRAFFIC. The shower sits opposite the room's entrance to keep its door swing from blocking access to other fixtures in the shared space.

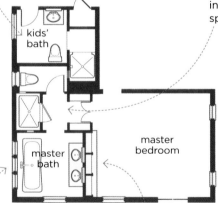

3 REWORK WINDOWS. The tub is tucked under three double-hungs in what used to be the master bedroom, for a light-drenched focal point opposite the console sinks.

4 INCREASE STORAGE. Built-in glass-front cabinets flank the bath's entryway. Shelves hold baskets for toiletries and other basics, plus family photos and artwork.

↑ Because you don't need to build a surround, a freestanding tub can be a cost-effective choice.

✱ DESIGN ADVICE

If you're on a tight budget, it pays to splurge on one eye-catching fixture, like a sculptural soaking tub, that can serve as a focal point.

the details

Clean lines and classic details capture the turn-of-the-century look

← ARCHES in the shower's doorway and interior tile details echo the bathtub's curves.

↑ THE CONSOLE SINK'S marble top sits on a nickel-finish, three-legged stand; horizontal supports double as towel bars.

EASY UPGRADE

Sinks with exposed metal console supports (and pipes) span the 1880s to the present, keeping baths open and airy and towels right at hand.

→ AN EXPOSED RISER topped by a rainhead brings a retro look to the shower. The wire corner basket is more modern but keeps soap and shampoo close at hand.

A vintage-style sunflower rainhead is a simple retrofit for an existing wall shower. →

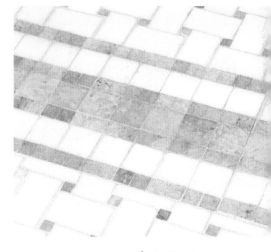

↑ MARBLE BASKETWEAVE TILE has period cred; the pale green accents match those found elsewhere in the house.

The old bathroom was so narrow that a person sitting on the toilet would bump knees against the tub.

before

ART DECO BATH

PROBLEM> The old bath had great period detail but was too far gone to restore.
SOLUTION> Keep the Deco style and re-create it with all-new fixtures and materials.

BUYING AN OLD HOUSE with an interior that hasn't been touched in more than half a century is a blessing and a curse. On one hand, you don't have to contend with someone else's taste in renovation. On the other hand, the original details may be so deteriorated that there's no salvaging them. Such was the case with this 1930s bath, which perfectly captured the era's Art Deco style but was laid to waste by decades of neglect.

So the owners decided to re-create it, using as many of the same products and materials as they could find. There were challenges, sure—old wall tiles, for instance, are thicker than what is commonly available today—but the problems inspired creative solutions. Rather than buy expensive custom or vintage tile, they used readily available stock subway tile and laid it in an extra-thick mortar bed to give it an old-fashioned look, then camouflaged the added thickness with bullnose cap molding laid over the top edge.

Along the way, they added 3 feet to the room's width, stolen from a hall closet, and relocated the fixtures for a more functional layout. Now they have a bath that's period-perfect, just like the old one, only a whole lot better.

after

The new bath, 3 feet wider and with fixtures repositioned, kept the black-and-white color scheme and Deco style of the original, but now it's clean, bright, and user-friendly.

An inset liner strip is an easy and affordable way to liven up plain white tile.
↓

↑
Need to fit a standard tub in a wide opening? A bumpout fills space and adds a handy ledge.

→ A BULLNOSE CAP MOLDING runs around the perimeter of the room and also wraps the beveled edges of the recessed vanity mirror.

EASY UPGRADE
A swath of color, like these red-painted walls, adds warmth to a space that doesn't get a lot of natural light and livens up a simple black-and-white palette.

the plan

Update an Art Deco bath while re-creating the best features of the original

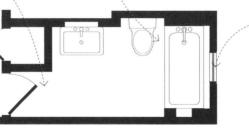

1 WIDEN THE ROOM. Stealing space from a hallway closet on the other side of the wall allowed the formerly cramped room to gain 3 feet in width.

2 TURN THE TUB. Before, the tub was opposite the sink and toilet. Moving it to the end of the room opened up floor space in the narrow bath.

3 MOVE THE WINDOW. The one existing window was moved from its former location in the corner so that it would be centered in the new tub alcove.

the details

Stock materials and creative touches rejuvenate a basic black-and-white bath

→ THE "SKYSCRAPER" SCONCES with black porcelain wall brackets are reproductions of a style typical in baths and kitchens of the 1930s.

A swing-out casement window allows for maximum ventilation in a humid area. →

↑A CASEMENT WINDOW replaced the former drafty double-hung on the shower wall. The leaded glass matches a window in the house's entry hall.

←A RECESSED NICHE is fitted with shelves made of the same marble that lines the ledge in the shower. Like the ledge, the niche exploits extra space behind the wall, created when the room was widened slightly.

Even a skylight couldn't keep the old bath—with its floral wallpaper, walnut-stained vanity, and buckling floor tiles—from feeling dark and drab.

before

VICTORIAN BATH

PROBLEM> Stained wood, dated fixtures, and drab styling made a 1970s-era bath dark and uninviting. **SOLUTION>** Lighten up the space with painted woodwork and a taupe-and-white color scheme.

WHEN A COUPLE OF EMPTY NESTERS set out to redo what had been their kids' hall bath, they wanted a vintage-inspired space that would complement their 1970s traditional brick house. With the children gone, it was their opportunity to create a luxurious extra bath, replacing the dark and dated fixtures with a classic claw-foot tub and a console sink.

But they also wanted all the modern amenities, like a separate glassed-in shower and plenty of storage. With its vintage style and taupe-and-white color scheme, the new bathroom not only fits right in with the rest of the house, it has a clean, inviting look—so much so that even though it was designed for guests, the homeowners use it all the time.

after

The new room is lighter and brighter, thanks to a neutral color palette and multiple wall sconces. The white-painted maple storage cupboard holds more than the old 10-foot-long vanity did and has glass knobs to keep the vintage look consistent.

The roomier a sink deck, the better. This one's 44 inches wide.
↓

Departing from black and white gives a hex-tile floor a fresh spin.
←

Varying materials—wood on one wall, tile on the other—help visually organize space.

the plan

Eliminate the wall-to-wall vanity and reposition fixtures to make space for a new tub and separate shower

1 **INCREASE STORAGE.** A 4-foot-wide-by-7-foot-high cupboard was built into an existing alcove.

3 **ADD A TUB.** The new freestanding tub sits across from the shower, in the space where the old toilet had been.

2 **REMOVE THE VANITY.** Getting rid of the wall-to-wall vanity allowed the rest of the fixtures to be repositioned. The toilet and a large console sink now occupy what was the vanity wall.

4 **SEPARATE THE SHOWER.** The combination tub/shower was replaced by a stall shower with a glass partition wall.

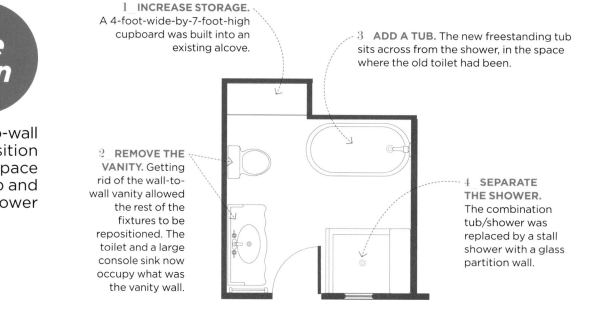

the details

Soft curves and neutral colors put an understated spin on Victorian exuberance

← A RECESSED NICHE makes clever use of wall space above the tub and keeps towels and bath products close at hand.

EASY UPGRADE

Create a "frame" around a wall niche with decorative tile trim in a contrasting color for a smart look that sets it off nicely against a white tiled wall.

↓ THE TURNED-LEG CONSOLE SINK, though new, looks like it was plucked from the past. A chrome faucet with porcelain lever handles adds to its period feel, as do the wood-framed medicine chest and reproduction sconces.

A ceiling-mounted rainhead keeps spray inside an open shower stall. →

↑ ONE CLEAR GLASS WALL and an open side help the shower— and the entire bathroom— seem larger.

→ THE CAST-IRON TUB'S sides and decorative claw feet are painted taupe to match the dominant floor tile color. The neutral tone creates a soft contrast to the mostly white fixtures.

Dress up exposed plumbing with decorative P-traps in a finish that matches the faucet.

CRAFTSMAN BATH

PROBLEM> Grown kids and their friends were crowding Mom and Dad out of the house.
SOLUTION> Convert the garage into living quarters, and add a luxurious bath in the unfinished attic.

AFTER THE KIDS MOVE OUT, most couples think about downsizing. But when the owners of this house found that their grown kids were frequently bringing friends home to an increasingly cramped dinner table, they realized they'd need more room than ever.

The subsequent rethinking of the home led to a renovation plan that included converting the old, attached garage into living space. While they were at it, they raised the garage's roof and used some of the unfinished attic for a separate guest suite. While the bedroom boasts a walk-in closet and lots of natural light, it's the bathroom—with its twin sinks, luxurious soaking tub, and treetop views—that's the real star of the space.

Following the homeowners' desire not to be "too country or too modern," the room gets its character from Craftsman-inspired details, such as mahogany-stained vanities, oil-rubbed bronze fittings, and stone-look ceramic tiles. The result is so comfortable and well appointed, it's a safe bet that the guest quarters will be booked by visiting family members for years to come, exactly as hoped.

after

With the roof of the attic bumped up, the new bath boasts an airy vaulted ceiling. Custom mahogany-stained, open-shelf vanity bases preserve the spacious feeling. Stained medicine cabinets echo the warm wood tones.

Capturing Craftsman style

TIPS FROM
SCOTT OMELIANUK
TOH EDITOR

When it comes to house styles, Craftsman is a hands-down favorite. In fact, when we polled readers, they voted for it over any other. The things that make it so appealing—natural wood tones, pleasing proportions, handcrafted character—look right at home with today's creature comforts. So even if you don't live in an early-1900s bungalow, you can still make Craftsman details work for you.

1 **Warm up with wood.** Early Craftsman houses owe much of their beauty to quartersawn oak and rich woodwork details. You can spot the influence here in the stained-mahogany vanities and molding-topped medicine cabinets.

2 **Embrace the handmade.** Even if you don't want to spring for individually made artisan tiles, there are plenty of manufactured products, such as the stone-look ceramic in this bath, that have the irregular appearance and rustic appeal of handmade versions. Ditto for oil-rubbed bronze fittings, which suggest a hand-forged look.

3 **Keep it simple.** Strong, unfussy lines and a palette of earth tones reinforce the Craftsman philosophy of natural materials, simply presented.

Open space at the top of a shower stall → allows steam to escape.

the plan

Renovate part of an unfinished attic to fit a spacious, amenity-filled guest bath

1 **ANNEX THE GARAGE.** Bumping up the roof and adding dormers on one side created enough space for living quarters.

2 **ADD HIS-AND-HERS VANITIES.** Twin sinks anchor the wall opposite the tub.

3 **CARVE OUT A SEPARATE TOILET ROOM.** With the toilet behind a pocket door, more than one guest can use the bathroom without sacrificing privacy.

to guest bedroom

mechanicals room

linen closet

↑**LARGE WINDOWS** and a frameless glass shower door maximize natural light and capture the treetop views.

4 **TUCK IN A SHOWER.** A frameless glass door maximizes natural light from the windows over the tub.

5 **CREATE A FOCAL POINT.** The tub takes center stage, while two large double-hung windows behind it offer views of the secluded backyard and the surrounding woods.

the details

Earthy tones, rustic tile, and oil-rubbed bronze accents impart Craftsman character

← **POCKET DOORS** are a Craftsman hallmark. These, in the toilet room, open to a linen closet that stores fresh towels and bedding for guests. Another set encloses the toilet room itself.

↓ **STONE-LOOK CERAMIC TILE** in muted taupe and beige adds to the warm, serene ambience of the space.

↓ **A RECESSED NICHE** in the shower is framed by a band of mosaic tile that echoes the border in the floor.

← **OIL-RUBBED BRONZE FITTINGS,** including the tub filler, sink faucets, and towel bars, are in keeping with the Craftsman-inspired decor.

CHAPTER 5

THE SALVAGE-STYLE BATH

Salvage yards are a treasure hunter's dream. These architectural warehouses, packed to the gills with old tubs, sinks, hardware, and lighting, make it easier than ever to find period elements to restore an old bath or put character into a new one without paying for custom work. There are a few caveats—some old fixtures can be tough to retrofit for today's plumbing codes—but with the help of our shopping tips, you can weed out the gems from the junk, and save a piece of building history from being tossed in the landfill while you're at it.

FLEA-MARKET FINDS, like this old dresser refitted for a vanity, can give a room instant character for minimal cost. An added benefit: With a piece that's already weathered, you don't have to worry about water spots.

IDEA FILE

Salvage yards and architectural antique shops are filled with great items that can add style to any bath. Here are just a few creative ways to use old finds

↑ THINK OUTSIDE THE BATH. A marble-topped barbershop washstand from the early 1880s perfectly captures turn-of-the-century style. Vintage subway tile, a salvaged toilet, and period glass shades on the original white ceramic wall sconces complete the picture.

The soakers of old have no faucet holes, so spouts must be wall- or floor-mounted.

← MAKE AN OLD TUB A FOCAL POINT. A 1913 tub sets the tone for a graceful bath. New subway tile wainscot and 1-inch hexagonal floor tiles are consistent with the era. A salvaged cabinet, painted white and fitted with bin pulls and latches, provides linen storage.

A circa-1940s dental cabinet provides storage with a bit of funky style.
↓

↑ADD A TWIST WITH COMMERCIAL FIXTURES.
Old house parts aren't the only things you'll discover at the salvage yard. You can also find great old details from office buildings and other institutional settings, like this beige marble wainscot, originally from San Francisco's Chevron building, and the pair of vitreous china janitor's sinks.

How to shop for salvage

TIPS FROM
AMY R. HUGHES, EDITOR, TOH "SALVAGE STYLE"

Salvage yards are famous for stockpiling vintage sinks, claw-foot tubs, and faucets. But plumbing fixtures are typically sold "as is," so make sure you check them out thoroughly before plunking down your cash. Here's what to look for.

1 **Bathtubs.** Avoid tubs with rust spots, dents, or missing feet, which are particularly hard to match. Make sure there's an adequately sized overflow drain—at least 2½ inches in diameter—to meet code and prevent floods.

2 **Sinks.** Consider space and installation constraints. Wall-mount sinks typically take up less room than pedestals, but they are heavy and require support in the wall framing. Porcelain sinks tend to be finer than enameled cast-iron ones and usually don't require refinishing.

3 **Faucets and fittings.**
Measure the distance between the centers of the faucet holes on your sink, and make sure any fittings you buy can fit this span. Avoid old faucet sets with missing parts, which are almost impossible to find. And unless you want to spend more money on replating than you do on the faucet itself, stay away from pitted chrome finishes.

↓ **CREATE FUNCTIONAL ACCENTS.** You can find porcelain cross-handle taps by the bucketful at the salvage yard for as little as $30 a pair. If you don't want to meddle with plumbing, you can still use them in the bath as towel racks or curtain tiebacks, putting some fun in functionality.

EASY UPGRADE
Cast-iron brackets are another versatile salvage-yard staple. Use them to hold up shelves, support a display rail, or create a stylish alternative to standard shelf brackets.

Stained glass is great in the bath because it allows light but blocks views. ←

↑ **DECORATE WITH ARCHITECTURAL ELEMENTS.** Architectural salvage doesn't necessarily have to perform its original function, like the carved wood corbel and facade details used here to give a new bath old-world flavor. The mirror over the 1930s-style Italian porcelain sink is made of old door casing and corner blocks.

← **REUSE OLD ACCENT WINDOWS.** Stained glass can instantly evoke an architectural style, whether it's a Queen Anne floral design or Arts and Crafts geometry. If you've got a modern, insulated window in the bath, you can hang a stained-glass panel in front of it, suspended from chains or hung on picture hooks.

↓ DON'T GIVE UP. It's hard to believe that the rusty old planter at left could ever be the centerpiece of a master bathroom. But after a professional refinishing and replacement of missing feet, the 90-year-old tub looks brand new and right at home surrounded by salvaged beadboard and old heart-pine flooring.

before

after

↑ The angled back of an old claw-foot is perfect for reclining, and a high overflow drain means a deeper soak.

TOH DESIGN ADVICE
You don't have to live in an old house to enjoy a claw-foot tub. Its sculptural curves can provide a welcome visual counterpoint to the angular lines of modern interiors.

DOUBLE SINKS make morning chat easy, provided you've got enough space. Allow at least 5 feet for a two-basin setup if you don't want to be bumping elbows with your mate.

CHAPTER 6>

THE HIS-AND-HERS BATH

For some couples, the morning and evening bathroom routines may be the most concentrated time they spend together. So a bath that functions for two is at the top of their wish list. But that doesn't mean they want the same things. Take sinks, for starters. A shared vanity is perfect for some people, while others prefer a separate but equal approach. Then there's the couple who went all the way: his-and-hers sinks, toilets, even two entrances to the shower. While that may be more than your space—and budget—allow, our examples show that you can still have a shared bath your own way.

before +afters

1_ **Side-by-Side Bath**

2_ **Zoned Bath**

3_ **Back-to-Back Bath**

Tucked into an 8½-by-17-foot space, the bath relies on freestanding sinks, lots of mirrors, and a high, windowed ceiling to preserve a feeling of openness. Recessed medicine cabinets and built-ins behind the sinks and on the opposite wall provide ample storage without taking up floor space.

SIDE-BY-SIDE BATH

PROBLEM> **One bath and low ceilings cramped a tall husband's style.**
SOLUTION> **Raise the roof to eke out more usable floor space for a new master bath.**

WITH THEIR LOW ROOFLINES, wainscoted walls, and built-in window seats, Arts and Crafts bungalows are cozy—sometimes too cozy. This 1916 Craftsman had three small bedrooms and one bath tucked into one-and-a-half stories. A narrow attic stair led to the second floor, where ceilings topped out at 7 feet under the ridgeline, making the upstairs bedroom and den barely usable. At 6-foot-2, the husband had to duck everywhere.

   With their sights set on expanding the family, the couple needed to turn that underperforming upper story into a functional space. So they bumped up the roof 7 feet, which freed up enough usable floor space to build a master suite. The resulting remodel features a two-part master bathroom that includes a half bath accessed from the hall, so that everyone won't have to converge at cleanup time. The little house is still snug, but these days it's a lot more comfortable.

Wall-to-wall mirroring visually doubles space, making snug quarters seem less so.
↓

Even a shallow built-in can add plenty of storage. This one's only 12 inches deep.
↑

→ **SALVAGED CARRIAGE DOORS** with cross-reeded glass hang from overhead tracks between the bedroom and bathroom, creating a unique connection between the spaces.

TOH DESIGN ADVICE
Textured glass in doors is a great way to let in light while still maintaining privacy.

the plan

Make a low-ceilinged second-story space functional and pleasant

1 RAISE THE ROOF. An additional 7 feet of clearance on the second floor made room for a new master bedroom and bath.

2 CREATE OPEN SPACE. Sliding doors unclutter the master suite, which has a hall through the middle of it.

3 SKIP THE TUB. Content to soak in the claw-foot tub on the first floor, the homeowners opted instead for a large, windowed shower.

4 CARVE OUT A BATH AND A HALF. The toilet room became a half bath that opens onto the hallway, so it can be shared by both upstairs bedrooms.

built-in cupboard

to master bedroom

the details

High ceilings, lots of light, and built-in storage expand a small space

→ **THE VAULTED CEILING** has twin skylights that fill the room with natural light. Pastel-painted walls add to the feeling of expansiveness.

Adding height gives a tight floor plan a lift (and raises spirits, too). ←

↑ **THE STEAM SHOWER** has three sets of controls consolidated on one wall, for the ceiling-mounted rainhead, wall shower, and hand shower. A granite-topped built-in bench sits near an awning window framed in water-resistant teak.

EASY UPGRADE

This shower gets its instant antique look from gray grout instead of white on the subway-tile walls and hex-tile floor.

→ **A BUILT-IN CUPBOARD** tucked next to the shower is detailed to look like a freestanding piece of furniture and holds toiletries and wardrobe overflow.

↑ Simple basket organizers keep toiletries accessible and clutter out of sight.

Strong horizontal lines can smooth out the sometimes choppy look of a bathroom.

before

Floral wallpaper and shiny brass faucets were out of sync with the rest of the 1920s-era house.

ZONED BATH

PROBLEM> The bath was dated and dysfunctional, but the fixtures couldn't be moved.
SOLUTION> Keep the footprint, give the space a facelift, and tailor the layout to the users' needs.

THE PERSONALITY—EVEN GHOST—of a home's former occupants often lingers most in the master bath. A floral Colonial specter haunted the bath in this 1920s house, whose owners were avid collectors of Arts and Crafts furniture. Apart from being a total mismatch with the rest of the place, the room had other problems: The heat was inadequate, and the standard-height vanities were too low for comfort (he's 6-foot-2, she's 5-foot-8).

Any plumbing changes would have meant tearing into the dining room below, with its beamed ceiling and Arts and Crafts wallpaper, so the design had to work with the existing fixture placement. But the footprint is the only thing that stayed the same. The handsomely remodeled bath now has plenty of heat, courtesy of a new radiator and electric radiant cables under the tile floor, plus custom-designed vanities that fit the owners. The Craftsman aesthetic—reflected in the color palette, tilework, and horizontal bands of oak trim—is more in keeping with the style of the home. And the frilly ghost is gone for good.

after

Earthy granite, wood cabinets, bronze fittings, and tiles with a handmade look give the new bath its Craftsman character.

→ **OAK TRIM** and bullnose molding make the mirror look like an old wall-hung medicine cabinet. The strong horizontal banding, echoed in the tile border, is a hallmark of Craftsman interiors.

the plan

Keep the location of the plumbing, but add new fixtures, heating, cabinets, and tile

1 OPTIMIZE COUNTER SPACE. The wife's granite-topped vanity stretches from wall to wall for a 5-foot-long sink deck.

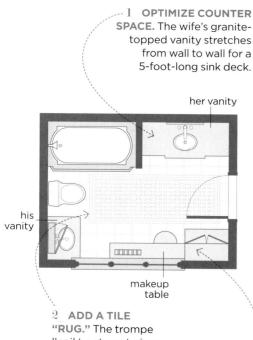

her vanity

his vanity

makeup table

2 ADD A TILE "RUG." The trompe l'oeil treatment gives the room's jagged perimeter a neat, unifying focal point.

3 BUILD IN STORAGE. A 7-foot-tall linen cupboard tucks into a corner, and a 4-foot-long makeup counter makes use of space under the window and over the radiator.

the details

Built-ins maximize storage and counter space while adding Craftsman style

↓ **A CAST-IRON RADIATOR** is tucked under the window and the makeup counter to warm the room—and take the chill off bare legs.

An illuminated mirror assures perfect lighting at any time of day.
↓

← **A BASKET-WEAVE TILE INSET** with a crisp rectangular border neatens up the edges of the room.

↑ **THE BUILT-IN LINEN CUPBOARD** has a granite counter that's higher than the adjoining makeup table to break up the mass and give both pieces the look of freestanding furniture.

Using the same flooring throughout the different areas of a divided space helps tie it together visually.
↓

A double-sided vanity and shower with two entrances define this as a shared space. But separate dressing areas and private WCs give each half of the couple a personal retreat.

BACK-TO-BACK BATH

PROBLEM> A busy couple wanted a space where they could be separate yet together. **SOLUTION>** Use a double-sided vanity to divide the room into his-and-hers privacy zones.

USUALLY, DOUBLE VANITIES ARE SIDE BY SIDE. Not this time. Instead of conventional twin sinks—or even separate sinks in opposite corners of the room—these homeowners opted for back-to-back vanities with sinks across from each other. That way, each one gets a private grooming area, but they can carry on a conversation in the morning.

The original plan called for the vanity to be a custom-built, furniture-style cabinet, but the wife spotted a pair of elegant bureaus at an antique shop, and brainstorming ensued. Six feet wide by 4½ feet deep, the fabricated vanity is an ingenious composition of the two dressers, placed back-to-back and topped with a slab of marble fitted with two undermount sinks.

Positioned roughly in the middle of the room, the vanity divides the space into distinct husband and wife domains. The shower, with two entrances, is accessible from both his side and hers via a pair of frameless glass doors. (The only tub, however, is decidedly on the wife's side.) Separate WCs and dressing closets complete the his-and-hers zoning.

→ **THE VANITY,** made from two antique bureaus, shares a common countertop and two-sided mirror. A heat lamp above each station provides post-shower warmth.

EASY UPGRADE
Taking out the top center drawer creates space in an old dresser to drop in an undermount sink; a false drawer front remains.

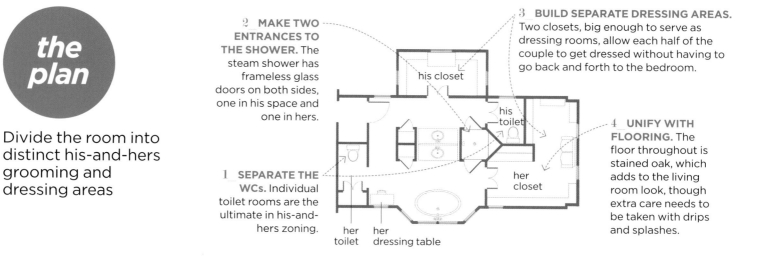

the plan

Divide the room into distinct his-and-hers grooming and dressing areas

2 MAKE TWO ENTRANCES TO THE SHOWER. The steam shower has frameless glass doors on both sides, one in his space and one in hers.

1 SEPARATE THE WCs. Individual toilet rooms are the ultimate in his-and-hers zoning.

his closet

his toilet

her closet

her toilet

her dressing table

3 BUILD SEPARATE DRESSING AREAS. Two closets, big enough to serve as dressing rooms, allow each half of the couple to get dressed without having to go back and forth to the bedroom.

4 UNIFY WITH FLOORING. The floor throughout is stained oak, which adds to the living room look, though extra care needs to be taken with drips and splashes.

the details Different wall treatments and furnishings give each space its own unique character

→ **THE VICTORIAN TUB,** on a wood pedestal, dominates the wife's side of the floor plan. Surrounding details give the space a living room look.

↑ **HIS SIDE** has its own entrance into the steam shower and a toilet room outfitted with cork wall covering and a hunt-cup table lamp.

↑ **THE DRESSING TABLE** is positioned to take advantage of natural light from a window above.

→ **HER SIDE** has a dressing table and its own wallpapered WC, which houses an antique book stand and a coat tree for hanging up bathrobes.

A LOW-COST, HIGH-STYLE design element, like this simple industrial cart fitted with a vessel sink, allows you to save while you splurge on a signature fixture, in this case a fancy tankless toilet.

CHAPTER 7 >
THE BUDGET BATH

We all want a luxe-looking washroom to suds up and shower in. The challenge is creating that spa-like space without getting soaked. But the budget-friendly baths you're about to see prove that it's not as hard as you might think. All it takes is some creativity with materials, a dash of design flexibility, and a willingness to be surprised. Throw in a little elbow grease, and we guarantee you'll get the polish you want at a price you can afford.

before
+afters

FIXED FOOTPRINT

PROBLEM> **The old apartment bath was a mess, and space was tight.**
SOLUTION> **Keep the footprint and fixture placement, and give it a classic redo.**

OLD DOESN'T ALWAYS mean quaint. Sometimes it just means dilapidated. The years hadn't been kind to this 1920s-era apartment bath: Chipped subway tiles lined the walls, rust spots marred the cast-iron sink, and concrete peeked out beneath the broken ceramic floor squares.

The surfaces were too far gone to restore, and the 5-by-11-foot space didn't allow for changing the fixture placement. So the homeowners decided to update every element but keep the vintage '20s look.

A new claw-foot tub and pedestal sink, old-fashioned faucets, and a black-and-white tile scheme ensured the room would lose none of its period charm. And some simple design tweaks, like replacing the square sink with a clipped-corner model and getting rid of the towel bars lining the wall, eased traffic in the tight quarters.

Now light, fresh, and clean, the rehabbed bath is a good example of how, with the right details, a small space can make a big statement.

after

A cast-iron tub, clean-lined pedestal sink, white subway tiles, and a black-and-white marble floor restore the classic early-20th-century look.

Light-reflecting beveled tile has a period look and helps a small space feel bigger.

↓

97

the plan

Rehabilitate every inch of a small apartment bathroom

1 KEEP THE FOOTPRINT.
The layout of the bath, with all the fixtures arrayed along a single wall, remained the same.

2 ADD FUNCTIONALITY.
Tiny tweaks, like a new pedestal sink with clipped corners, ease movement in the small room.

3 USE EVERY AVAILABLE SPACE.
A towel bar mounted behind the curved end of the tub keeps bath sheets at the ready.

→ THE SHOWER CURTAIN is suspended from a ring attached to the ceiling. In a setup like this, where the freestanding tub also functions as a shower stall, you need some way to create an enclosure. This tub has only a handheld shower, but ceiling-mounted enclosures often attach to a plumbing riser with a fixed showerhead.

Freshly tiled walls, a new coat of paint, and old-fashioned fixtures update an early-20th-century classic

← **A HAND-TOWEL HOOK** built into the wall-hung soap dish saves space in the sink area and adds to the room's period feel.

↑ **A WALL-MOUNT TUB FILLER** with its own hand shower makes hair washing (and tub cleaning) much easier.

← **TILE BASEBOARD** was fashioned by turning field tiles on end and topping them with trim for a custom look at minimal added cost.

Low-cost tile tricks

TIPS FROM
COLETTE SCANLON, TOH DESIGN EDITOR

We love the clever baseboard in this bath—wall tile turned sideways to create a custom look with stock materials. Because tile comes in so many styles and colors, it's one of the easiest ways to add visual impact without shelling out extra money. Here are some more of our favorite budget-stretching tile tricks.

1 **Top a wall of wainscot.** You can still fit a luxe material into the budget if you use it sparingly and for maximum effect. For instance, try adding a row of patterned ceramic tile on top of plain field tile or simple beadboard wainscoting to create a dramatic top border.

2 **Vary the patterns.** A plain material takes on a more interesting and sophisticated look if you use it in a variety of ways. For example, lay tile in a square grid halfway up the shower wall, cap it with a tiled rail, then continue installing the tile on the diagonal—you'll get a more decorative effect.

3 **Break up the field.** Something as simple and inexpensive as creating a pencil border around the room with a line of thin tiles instantly boosts an ordinary design into one that's classic and elegant.

Cracked floor tiles and an old laminate vanity made the tiny upstairs bath seem dirty. **before**

STYLE ON A SHOESTRING

PROBLEM> **The budget didn't allow for a full bathroom makeover.**
SOLUTION> **Use surplus materials and get creative with stock.**

SOMETIMES STAYING FLEXIBLE is the key to renovation success. In this case, it's how one homeowner was able to afford her bath's dramatic cosmetic overhaul on a modest $4,000 budget.

She wasn't planning a full renovation of the small upstairs bath, just some cosmetic tweaks, like getting rid of the rust-stained tub and cracked tile floor, which always looked dirty no matter how often she scrubbed. But when her contractor offered a stash of marble tile left over from another job—at less than half its market price—she quickly said yes, even though yellow wasn't her first choice of color. The result: a luxe-looking bath on a shoestring budget.

Another money-saving decision, to keep the 18-inch-deep cast-iron tub and have it professionally cleaned, was a winner too. The stylistic gamble paid off. Now the room is a golden-toned retreat, made all the richer by how little it cost.

after

Now it's as good as gold, with floors and walls of tumbled yellow marble and a warm-toned maple vanity.

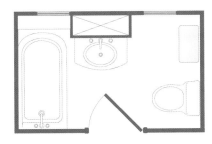

← A STOCK VANITY gets a personalized look from $25 worth of painted metal knobs that the homeowner added.

SMART SAVE

Keeping fixtures in place is the surest way to keep costs down. New sconces went right where the old ones were.

↑ Here's a space-saver for a shallow vanity: Use a TP holder instead of a hand-towel bar.

↑FRESH WHITE PAINT cleaned up the existing radiator cover. Chair rail molding, also painted white, was nailed directly on top of the plain strip that already wrapped the room.

← PAINTING THE CAST-IRON TUB was a cheaper alternative than building a surround. The contractor painted the exposed sides with acrylic latex and filled a gap in front with wallboard.

IDEA FILE

We're all looking to improve what we've got without forking over a fistful of cash. Here's what you can do with tile, paint, and vintage finds to get made-to-order looks at off-the-shelf prices

→ SCORE A VINTAGE WASHSTAND. Set between matching pedestal sinks, a tiled-back washstand creates a his-and-hers vanity for a lot less coin than a new dresser-style model. Similar pieces can be had for a couple of hundred bucks at antique stores or thrift shops. A tiled border dresses up inexpensive wood beadboard.

↓ WARM UP WITH RUSTIC ACCENTS. Weathered barn-board shelves help complete the look of a relaxed retreat for a fraction of the cost of new storage units. Rejuvenate an old claw-foot tub by painting the outside with a metal-safe enamel. Here, a serene palette of watery hues on the walls is complemented by a soft gray paint on the tub exterior.

↑ TURN A SIDEBOARD INTO A VANITY. A flea-market buffet with mirrored back can replace both a run-of-the-mill medicine chest and a sink cabinet. Paint it the same color as the walls to give it the look of a built-in.

Don't want to pay for a custom tile pattern? This one was applied using epoxy paint.
↓

For a vintage feel, make a divider from salvaged windows or shutters. →

↓ USE LUXE MATERIALS CREATIVELY. Mix small quantities of discounted odd-lot hexagonal mosaic tiles, skinny "liners," and oversize subway tiles to create a distinctive vertical backsplash for less than half the cost of a custom tile order.

↑ GO FOR DIVIDERS INSTEAD OF WALLS.
An airy and open design translates to lower construction costs. A translucent room divider like this one, made from stock acrylic panels, creates a visual partition without blocking natural light. Open storage is more budget friendly than closed cabinetry, too. Here, a wood-lined niche at the end of the tub makes a convenient cubby for towels—and also looks a lot better than a plumbing access door.

← **PRETEND YOU'RE OUTSIDE.** Outdoor-shower paneling from the lumberyard, nailed to vertical framing, makes a unique vanity cabinet. (Mahogany 1x4s are a stable wood choice in wet areas.) Open shelves rest on cleats screwed to the wall. An outdoor utility light continues the theme and offers plenty of style and illumination for a lot less than a dressy sconce. A soapstone vanity top, with its river-rock color and natural finish, has a warmer look—and a lower price tag—than polished marble or granite.

A simple wood dowel makes a great TP holder and costs just a buck. ←

TOH DESIGN ADVICE

If you're shopping for a vanity top, visit a stone yard to see what scraps they might have left over from a larger job. Since there isn't much use for 22-by-28-inch slabs, you can usually talk the supplier into giving you a good deal on high-end materials, which they'll also cut to your specifications.

→ **CUSTOMIZE A CHAIR RAIL.** Set plain subways on end to create a dentil-style border on tiled wainscot. Seal the exposed, unglazed ends with caulk.

← **CREATE HANDCRAFTED CHARACTER.** A simple gingham curtain works wonders. Hung on a plain rod, the cheerful fabric hides exposed plumbing and punches up an otherwise monochromatic color scheme. It also adds some under-sink storage space.

EASY UPGRADE

Add a demilune backsplash to a plain vanity to give it the look of a vintage washstand.

←THROW IN BOLD ACCENTS. Scatter accent tiles in a different color or material within a wall of moderately priced field tiles. Here, glass subways punctuate plain white ceramic rectangles. You can achieve the same effect by interspersing smaller handmade or mosaic tiles.

→RECYCLE BUILDING MATERIALS. Give a plain-Jane bath a bit of well-worn character with repurposed building elements. These distressed painted boards, originally wainscot from a 1920s kitchen, instantly transform a basic bath into something special. The wall treatment adds practicality, too, by providing a convenient shelf for toiletries and display items.

A TUB WITH A VIEW can turn everyday bathing into an indulgent experience. The generously proportioned pedestal tub assures a deep, relaxing soak, and the graceful curves of the floor-mounted tub filler add period style.

CHAPTER 8>
THE TAKE-ME-AWAY BATH

A refuge from the outside world, a romantic hideaway at home, and a retreat as pampering as any resort—that's the recipe for a take-me-away bath. Fill it with amenities like a generous soaking tub or whirlpool bath, a steam shower, even a fireplace, and who needs a spa vacation? The examples on the following pages may be long on luxury, but they're also filled with good ideas you can use to turn any size bath into your own private getaway. The only thing missing are fluffy robes and room service.

before +afters

1_ **Center Stage**

2_ **Fire and Water**

3_ **Modern Master**

4_ **Tub With a View**

Because a tub doesn't take up upper wall space, use it as an opportunity to add windows.
↓

before

Narrow windows, dingy tiles, mirrored walls, and leaky pipes made the 1980s-style bath redo feel uninviting and out of sync with the house's period architecture.

CENTER STAGE

PROBLEM> The 1980s bath was dingy, the plumbing leaked, and the decor didn't suit a 1908 home.
SOLUTION> Bump out the space, create a dramatic focal point, and add a vintage look.

ONE THING CAN LEAD TO ANOTHER when a remodel is under way. The owners of this sunlit master bath were embarking on some changes to the Shingle-style home they'd lived in for two years when the architect made a suggestion: Instead of the simple cosmetic update they'd planned for their leaky, '80s-style bath, why not go a bit further? With a small addition, she explained, they could get the upgrade they wanted, plus a lot more storage and treetop views.

The plan hinged on a modest bumpout—about 8 feet deep and 10½ feet wide—to allow for twin vanities and a vaulted, windowed bay for a freestanding tub, positioned to maximize river views. The original section of the bathroom now holds a shower, a dressing area with custom cabinets, and a private toilet room, a detail the homeowners are grateful for, since one of their teenage daughters likes to use the space too. "She has her own bath," says her father, "but she says ours is superior now."

after

The sculptural 6-foot tub, elevated on a platform in the new windowed bay, soaks up natural light and scenic vistas.

An overhead vanity fixture should be wide enough to cast even light over the user's face. →

WARDROBE CABINETS flank a built-in vanity table, creating a dressing area and adding storage space for the master suite.

the plan

Turn a dated, uncomfortable bath into a soothing space with ample storage and spectacular views

1   **BUMP OUT.** Adding about 80 square feet at the far end of the bath created a large windowed bay to hold the freestanding tub with built-in vanities on either side.

2   **ELEVATE THE TUB.** Raising it up one step afforded a clear sight line to river views.

3   **INCREASE PRIVACY.** A separate toilet room has its own door.

4   **RELOCATE THE SHOWER.** Moving it to where the linen closet was allowed for a larger footprint.

5   **CREATE A DRESSING AREA.** A vanity table flanked by floor-to-ceiling wardrobe cabinets now fills the wall where the tub and shower once stood.

the details

Lots of light, gentle curves, and soft colors add up to a look of understated elegance

↑ **VERDE LAGUNA MARBLE** lines the luxurious shower stall, which has a curved wall, a glass door, and built-in bench seating.

↑ **MATCHING STONE-TOPPED VANITIES,** one at either end of the tub, take advantage of the generous light from the new bay window.

← **POLISHED-CHROME** tub and shower fittings honor the home's turn-of-the-century vintage.

← **TINY GLASS MOSAICS** ring the shower stall, forming a border between marble tiles above and ceramic below.

A '70s classic, the bath had garish shag carpeting, gaudy metallic wallpaper, dim light, and a bad layout.

FIRE AND WATER

PROBLEM> The '70s-era bath was voted "America's Ugliest."
SOLUTION> Gut it, bump out 3 feet, and add a beachy feel.

THE HOMEOWNERS DREAMED OF a luxurious master bath with his-and-hers vanities, a glassed-in shower, and a relaxing whirlpool tub set before a cozy fireplace. The problem was figuring out how their current bathroom could be turned into their vision. The space hadn't been touched since the 1970s and still had the DayGlo shag carpeting and metallic orange-and-yellow wallpaper to prove it. The bathroom was so repulsive that the couple entered it in American Standard's "America's Ugliest Bathroom" contest—and won.

They put their winnings to work and reconfigured the 10-by-12-foot galley layout into the bath they wanted. By bumping out one wall nearly 3 feet and changing the floor plan, they were able to fit in all the upgrades, including larger windows, accessible storage, and a connecting door to the bedroom. With its luxurious finishes and soothing colors inspired by the owners' love of the beach, what was once the nation's ugliest is now a real winner.

The centerpiece of the remodeled bath is a 6-foot whirlpool tub with a marble deck and a custom-painted pine surround. The two-sided gas fireplace, trimmed in mosaic tiles that evoke beach glass, can also be enjoyed from the adjoining master bedroom.

For that beach-cottage feel, nothing beats a paneled ceiling.

For a fun look, run shower tiles vertically to echo the effect of falling water. ↓

FURNITURE-STYLE BUILT-INS take advantage of every inch of available storage. Tiny bun feet create toekick space and lighten the look of the cabinets.

EASY UPGRADE

To trick the eye into thinking a space is larger than it actually is, use wall-to-wall mirrors, see-through shower partitions, and neutral colors.

the plan

Transform a small galley into a bigger, brighter space with a spa-like feeling

1 **ENLARGE THE SPACE.** Encroaching 32 inches into the bedroom allowed the old 10-by-12-foot bath to accommodate a new layout.

2 **CREATE STORAGE.** A closet for clothes and linens adds accessible storage for the bath and adjoining bedroom.

3 **ADD A TUB.** Keeping the tub deck to a narrow 3 inches made it possible to fit in the 6-foot whirlpool soaker.

4 **IMPROVE LIGHTING.** Two fixed-glass trapezoidal windows were enlarged, and an awning window replaced an old horizontal slider.

5 **ADD A SECOND SINK.** His-and-hers vanities flank the corner shower. Hers has an extra-wide deck to serve as a makeup area.

the **details**

Luxurious touches and soothing colors add to the bath's sophistication and comfort

↓ **TUMBLED-GLASS MOSAIC** tiles line a recessed shower niche edged with matching subway tiles.

→ **POLISHED CHROME TUB FIXTURES** include a convenient hand shower. The fireplace surround is made of the same tumbled-glass mosaic tiles as the shower niche.

→ **CHROME HANDLES** placed perpendicular to each other on opposite sides of the shower door add visual impact. On the outside, the 18-inch horizontal handle doubles as a towel bar.

↑ **RIVER-ROCK TILES** in the shower come on mesh sheets for easy installation. The frameless glass corner shower is designed to make the most of the enlarged—yet still relatively compact—floor plan.

To avoid "clumps" of color, test-fit variegated tiles before committing to a layout. ↓

MODERN MASTER

PROBLEM> **A couple of outdoor sports lovers got tired of fighting over the shower.**
SOLUTION> **Reshuffle rooms to make a two-person bath with a spa-like feeling.**

YOU WORK OUT, you sweat, you hop in the shower. But if both of you work out and sweat—well, then you fight for the shower. Which is why the flashpoint of many busy households is the wait to get under the hot water. One couple of admitted gym rats and outdoor sports enthusiasts solved that problem when they built a shower for two as part of a large-scale bath renovation.

Annexing a section of a second-floor roof deck, they created a spacious 10-by-19-foot master bath that accommodates two sinks along a 10-foot stretch of countertop plus two dressing closets. "Our goal was room to move," says the husband. "We were used to bumping into each other in the bathroom."

They had a few other items on their wish list for the new space. He wanted to see the outdoors from a multispray shower; she wanted a clean, modern look. They agreed on the use of rich, natural materials: highly textured, mottled slate tiles for the floor; limestone on the walls; and a mix of maple cabinets and mahogany millwork. The couple also insisted the space usher in the outdoors as much as possible. So they added twin skylights, suspended a mirror over each basin that allows the window behind to peek through, and installed a sliding door to the deck. All of which amplify natural light—as well as the sunset view while showering after an evening run.

after

A pair of skylights and organic materials—limestone walls, a gray slate countertop, maple and mahogany woodwork, and a multicolor, cleft-slate floor—invite nature indoors.

THE LIMESTONE SHOWER is partially enclosed in frameless glass to preserve the view outside. In addition to two showerheads and multiple body sprays, the 5-by-8-foot shower has twin built-in corner seats and wall niches for toiletries.

the plan

Enclose part of a deck to make room for a spa-like master bath

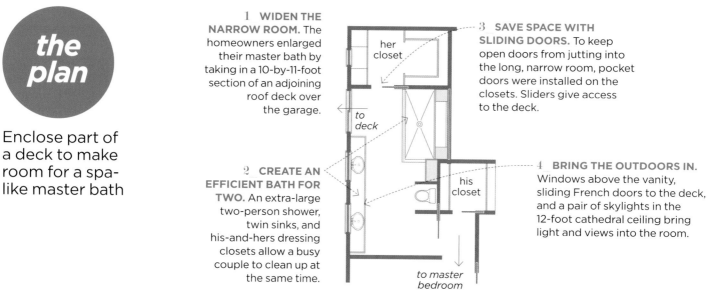

1 **WIDEN THE NARROW ROOM.** The homeowners enlarged their master bath by taking in a 10-by-11-foot section of an adjoining roof deck over the garage.

2 **CREATE AN EFFICIENT BATH FOR TWO.** An extra-large two-person shower, twin sinks, and his-and-hers dressing closets allow a busy couple to clean up at the same time.

3 **SAVE SPACE WITH SLIDING DOORS.** To keep open doors from jutting into the long, narrow room, pocket doors were installed on the closets. Sliders give access to the deck.

4 **BRING THE OUTDOORS IN.** Windows above the vanity, sliding French doors to the deck, and a pair of skylights in the 12-foot cathedral ceiling bring light and views into the room.

the **details**

Natural materials, lots of light, and open views create an outdoorsy feeling

↓ **A MAHOGANY-FRAMED POCKET DOOR** into the closet keeps the narrow bath uncluttered. A mirror extends the space as it reflects light and views.

↑ **A FRAMED MIRROR** is suspended from the window casing above each vessel sink to guard privacy yet let a glimpse of the outdoors peek through.

TOH DESIGN ADVICE

If you're installing a steam shower, make it big enough for two. That way you can share some relaxation time in a world that doesn't often allow it.

after

A little-used porch is now a luxurious retreat for soaking in the tub or curling up in a chair and enjoying the wraparound water views. A 1930s gilded glass mural, moved from the old master bath, provides a decorative backdrop.

TUB WITH A VIEW

PROBLEM> The master bath wasn't big enough for both a tub and a separate shower.
SOLUTION> Turn an unused porch into a garden-style bathing room.

MOST HOUSES CAN'T BOAST a view-filled room dedicated solely to bathing and relaxing. But for one couple, turning a little-used porch off their master bedroom into a private tub room meant they could have it all: a conventional master bath with a power shower for quick daily washups, and a luxurious retreat for leisurely soaks.

The house's existing master bath was dark and outdated. Like many busy working folks, the couple wanted a new bath equipped with amenities that would add efficiency to their morning routines—double sinks, two medicine cabinets, a spacious shower with two heads, and a separate WC. But they also wanted a tub for relaxing after a long day.

Space constraints forced a choice: bathtub or shower? The porch, with its second-story vantage point overlooking a sparkling bay, provided the perfect answer. At the center of the space, a 6-foot-long whirlpool tub is treated like an ornamental garden pool, with a limestone deck and paneled surround. Now, instead of one dark and outdated master bath, the couple has a bright, two-room master that gives them everything they wanted—and a whole lot more.

Grid patterns help create a sense of intimacy amid openness.
↓

Illumination from beneath adds to the "floating" effect— and also provides night lights. ↓

FLOATING DOUBLE VANITIES keep the floor uncluttered. Ceiling-high mirrors conceal oversize medicine cabinets.

the plan

Update the master bath, and create a light-filled tub room on the old porch

1 **CREATE A BATHING/ SITTING ROOM.** An unheated porch off the master bedroom was gutted and plumbed; the floor was leveled and shored up with new beams to support a whirlpool tub.

2 **ADD STORAGE.** The old dressing area, two steps up from the main bath, was fitted with a wall of closets that still leaves plenty of space for getting dressed.

3 **EXPAND THE FOOTPRINT.** Stealing a foot of space from an extra bedroom allowed for the addition of a 3-by-6-foot shower and a second window. The separate WC is behind a pocket door.

bathing/ sitting room

master bedroom

dressing room

the details

Traditional styling stays open and airy with clean lines and lots of light

↑ HAMMERED NICKEL UNDERMOUNT SINKS provide a textural contrast to the smooth limestone decking. Traditionally styled polished nickel faucets with lever handles complete the picture.

↑ THE 3-BY-6-FOOT SHOWER is built for two, with a small rainhead and a handheld nozzle next to the built-in bench. The all-glass enclosure keeps the room clean and open. A wall-mounted unit warms towels within reach of the shower door.

✳ TOH DESIGN ADVICE
Use common materials to visually link separate spaces. Here, the same limestone that lines the floor and sink decks is used for the tub surround on the former porch.

CHAPTER 9

THE MOSTLY WHITE BATH

White looks clean, white feels fresh. So it's no wonder white is the go-to color for bathrooms. But there are as many ways to design a mostly white bath as there are shades of white—and as you'll see, there are an awful lot. White looks good with every color, and that chameleon quality means it works in any type of space, from formal to casual, traditional to playful. And unlike some other color choices, which may have seemed like a good idea at the time, white never goes out of style.

A MAN'S BATH gets its clean, simple character from an all-white color scheme. An inset of dark green glass tiles on the floor and in the steam shower helps define the room's bathing and grooming spaces. Mixing materials—wood on the walls, tile on the floor and in the shower—keeps the monochrome palette from becoming monotonous.

IDEA FILE

White can set the tone for just about any kind of space, from rustic to luxurious—so whatever mood you want to create, there's a right white for you

↑ **WARM AND RUSTIC** A tone-on-tone bath puts the focus on variations in materials and textures, like the wood paneling and stone wainscot here. Against the light background, the double-wide trough sink, with its dark exterior, looks like a piece of wall-mounted sculpture.

The variations in handmade tiles add interest to a white wall.

← **CRISP AND CLEAN** A classic black-and-white bath is timeless. This one gets a modern update from a checkerboard tile inset in the shower. The curvy lines of the porcelain console sink and chrome faucet provide a nice visual counterpoint to the geometric patterns on the walls and floor.

↓ **RICH AND LUXURIOUS** White-painted cabinetry highlights a luxurious material, in this case the Carrara marble with elaborate edge detailing that tops a wall-to-wall vanity. The built-in unit, inspired by an antique hutch, has open shelves in the base cabinets to relax the formal styling.

Items on view in open shelves bring color and texture into a monochrome scheme. ↓

Picking the right white

The single most popular paint color in the world might also be the most confounding. One problem is that there are so many variations of the hue. Most whites are either "warm" or "cool." To figure out which is right for your space, test a few different shades to see how they work with the other colors at play in the room.

1 **Warm whites** incorporate an undertone of yellow—think French vanilla ice cream—or a touch of rust, pink, or brown. Warm colors appear to advance, so a creamy white can make a large space seem cozier.

2 **Cool whites** have green, blue, or gray undertones. Crisp and clean-looking, they lend themselves to modern spaces. Because cool colors appear to recede, a cool white can visually expand a small room.

3 **Pure whites** are the whitest whites of all, formulated with few or no tinted undertones. So-called clean whites are most often used on ceilings, to create a neutral field above and visually lift the ceiling height.

ceiling bright white

pearly white

ibis white

antique white

pure white

A favorite artwork becomes a star on a white wall (just make sure it can take the humidity). ↓

TOH DESIGN ADVICE

Follow the same rules for painting with white as for any other color: Choose two or three shades, put up test swatches, and eyeball them during the day and night.

↓**ROMANTIC** A palette of soft whites makes a cottage-style bath feel cozy and serene. Visual interest comes from the variety of patterns—hex tiles on the floor, vertical beadboard and horizontal paneling on the walls—while the rugs, towels, and furnishings add color and texture. An abundance of light through the French doors and skylight ensures that the creamy whites will look rich instead of dingy.

↑**CLASSIC** A Greek key floor pattern takes center stage in a traditional bath. The homeowner laid out the design himself, using reference books to nail the period look for the 1918 house. Gray grout gives the floor a timeworn appearance and helps it stand out against the white wainscot. Wall-mounted votive holders in the tub area add a modern twist.

→ **TRADITIONAL** The classic turn-of-the-century bath gets its characteristic look from light marble-topped console sinks and clean-looking expanses of tile. The dark built-in cupboard provides contrast to balance all the white and keeps the dominant color from feeling boring.

← **MODERN** Clean, crisp whites go well with cool blues and lend themselves to contemporary spaces. This simple and bright bath serves as a showcase for a special material on the vanity top and tub surround: slabs of concrete embedded with glittering flecks of crushed glass from recycled bottles.

Eased edges are better than sharp corners where space is tight. →

ADDING A BATH where none existed before allows you to get creative with the floor plan, as in this bumped-up space that houses a salvaged claw-foot tub and open shower lined in honed black slate.

CHAPTER 10 >

THE BONUS BATH

Sometimes you're lucky enough to have a space in the house where you can add an extra bath. Then the challenge becomes adapting a quirky location—say, a low-ceilinged attic or a windowless garage—into a bath that functions well and blends in with the rest of the home's architecture. One secret is to make the quirks work in your favor. Stuck with a long, skinny space? Think vertically! That's how one family hit on the idea of a raised tub platform that turned a former home office into a showcase bath. These examples prove that with a little creativity you can transform even the most uninviting space into a bath you'll love.

before +afters

1_ **Drive-in Bath**

2_ **Attic Bath**

3_ **Bumpout Bath**

Task, ambient, and natural lighting are the perfect bath combo.

Radiant heat is the best way to make a stone floor bare-feet friendly.

before The garage hadn't been home to a car in some time and was being used as a home office and storage area.

DRIVE-IN BATH

PROBLEM> The master bath was a tight squeeze for parents and kids.
SOLUTION> Relocate it to a roomy garage area that wasn't being used for cars.

NOT ALL MID-CENTURY RAMBLERS have rooms that ramble. Take this 1961 ranch house, for example. Morning traffic jams in the 5-by-8-foot master bath got so bad that the homeowners decided it was time for a spacious update, especially after a toddler and an infant had entered the bath-time rotation.

To realize their vision of an amenity-filled master bath—he wanted a shower enclosure lined in shimmering glass tile, she wanted a deep soaking tub—they annexed the space occupied by a garage-turned-home-office. Along the way, they traded the garage's boxy footprint for gently curving walls, to take full advantage of the light-reflecting properties of all that iridescent glass tile.

The new 13-by-17-foot master bath has a floating double vanity, a shower with four watery-blue shades of tile cascading down the walls, and a tub large enough to bathe both kids at once. And, best of all, no fender benders to start the day.

after

An iridescent bronze finish on the glass-tile wall lightens up the room, as does the double vanity that appears to float in space above a marble tile floor.

the plan

Reshape the new space and place the fixtures so that there's plenty of room to move

1 THROW A CURVE. The old garage formed a perfect square. The new front wall is curved to soften the previously boxy footprint.

2 ADD CURVES INSIDE, TOO. Walls with rounded edges enclose the shower and the toilet, bouncing light off the glass mosaic tile.

3 LET IN LIGHT WHILE PRESERVING PRIVACY. Square casement windows high on the wall above the tub and shower brighten the room without providing a view to what's inside.

4 SPREAD OUT FIXTURES. Maintaining empty space between the cleanup stations makes the room feel larger. The shower and toilet, in their own enclosures, are screened from the tub.

A DEEP SOAKING TUB is the star of the space. Its clean lines are set off by a backdrop of rectangular bronze-glazed black tiles made from recycled bottles.

the details

Sinuous lines and shimmering surfaces create a soothing, spa-like feel

→ **RIBBONLIKE FITTINGS** keep the look streamlined. Wall mounting clears the sink deck and adds to the open feeling.

Clear glass tiles require careful installation, since flaws in the wall behind will be on display, too.
↓

↑ **CONTEMPORARY TRACK LIGHTING** bounces light off the walls, washing them with a soft glow. Beige paint adds to the warmth.

← **THE WATERFALL EFFECT** in the shower was custom designed with the aid of a computer. To make installation easy, the tiles come premounted on 11-by-12-inch sheets.

With the addition of a basin sink, virtually any furniture piece can be turned into a vanity.

before The unfinished attic wasn't being used for much besides storage. A bathroom, updated in the 1960s, was dirty and deteriorated.

ATTIC BATH

PROBLEM> **The old attic bath had a makeshift layout—and decades of grime.**
SOLUTION> **Gut it, rearrange the fixtures, and add period details.**

MANY AN OLD HOUSE comes with evidence of a not-quite-as-old renovation. When the owners of this home moved in, they took one look at the attic bath's circa-1960 "update" and closed the door—for five years. There was a filthy metal shower in the middle of the room, a tiny sink and toilet crammed into one corner, and layers of vinyl peeling off the floor.

The family focused their attention on other areas of the Queen Anne until, finally, the lack of a bath near the kids' attic playroom became too inconvenient to bear. They gutted the space, literally throwing the shower out the window. Then the designer who was working downstairs on the couple's kitchen renovation came up for a look. He helped them determine the layout and sketched the panel-molding ceiling treatment. The rest of the design ideas were the wife's, culled from years of clipping magazines like *This Old House* and taking pictures of favorite architectural elements.

The new attic bath mixes old-house detail with modern elements and vintage finds. Now the thoughtfully renovated space fits the character of the house, and the family has a much-needed third bath.

after

The new space is fresh and inviting. Panel molding on the vaulted ceiling sports crisp, reflective paint, and a mix of old and new elements suits the character of the house.

THE CLAW-FOOT TUB is flanked by a pair of storage niches recessed between the wall studs.

SMART SAVE

As a less costly alternative to salvaged planks, you can distress new flooring to make it look old. Contractors battered these new white-oak planks with chains.

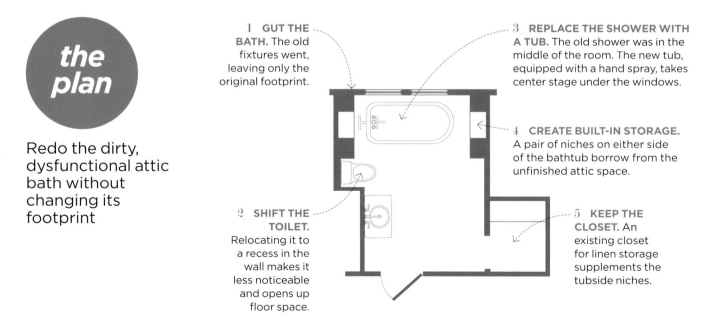

the plan

Redo the dirty, dysfunctional attic bath without changing its footprint

1 **GUT THE BATH.** The old fixtures went, leaving only the original footprint.

2 **SHIFT THE TOILET.** Relocating it to a recess in the wall makes it less noticeable and opens up floor space.

3 **REPLACE THE SHOWER WITH A TUB.** The old shower was in the middle of the room. The new tub, equipped with a hand spray, takes center stage under the windows.

4 **CREATE BUILT-IN STORAGE.** A pair of niches on either side of the bathtub borrow from the unfinished attic space.

5 **KEEP THE CLOSET.** An existing closet for linen storage supplements the tubside niches.

Traditional style mixes with modern convenience, and vintage pieces add plenty of character

→ **WINDOW CASINGS** with pilaster details link the bath to the rest of the 1898 house. The style was modeled after the woodwork in the homeowner's previous residence.

↑ **ANTIQUE FINDS,** such as this Chinese chest inlaid with mother-of-pearl, get an update from new elements, like a marble vessel sink and wall-mounted pewter fittings.

Backing niches with mirrors is a clever way to add interest and maximize light.

↑ **A NICKEL TUB FILLER** with a hand spray lets the bathtub do double duty in a space that doesn't have a separate shower.

EASY UPGRADE
Old mirrors have mottled wear patterns that add interest and character. Such pieces are not hard to find; this one came from the stash of a local glass-and-mirror supplier.

← **RAISED-PANEL BASEBOARDS** echo the ceiling treatment. The wide, white-painted woodwork lightens the space and provides a crisp contrast to the distressed oak floor.

This second-floor home office at the rear of the house, overlooking the yard and an adjoining horse farm, had great views but didn't get much use.

before

BUMPOUT BATH

PROBLEM> **Five people at home...and only one-and-a-half baths.**
SOLUTION> **Turn a seldom-used upstairs office off the master bedroom into a roomy new master bath.**

CHOP UP A NARROW SPACE to make it feel bigger? It may sound counter-intuitive, but that's just what made this master bath seem more expansive.

The space started out as a seldom-used office at the rear of the house, adjacent to the master bedroom. Faced with the long, rectangular layout, the designer suggested separating the bath into two rooms: one for his-and-hers sinks and a claw-foot soaking tub, the other for the shower and toilet. To open it up even more, an adjacent dressing closet was reworked with a doorway into the bath, creating an uninterrupted sight line from one end of the space to the other.

And what a sight line it is. The tub, nestled into a new bay window alcove created by bumping out 3 feet onto an existing wooden deck, offers bucolic views of the yard and adjoining horse farm. Two entrances from the bedroom create a circular flow; white woodwork and warm beige walls, plus plenty of windows—six in all—give the compact rooms an airy, open feel.

after

Now the views are the star of the space. A new bay window alcove, bumped out 3 feet onto the upper deck, is the perfect place for a claw-foot soaking tub.

The tub's "stage" also hides plumbing and wiring.

↓

→ **AN OLD-FASHIONED PEDESTAL SINK,** a wall-mounted wood medicine chest, and a glass-shaded wall sconce help the bath look like it's always been there. The wide-plank pine floors are painted white to match those in the master bedroom.

SMART SAVE

A wall-mounted medicine cabinet not only captures the period look, it's also an easy installation because the wall doesn't have to be opened.

A light color scheme makes a small space feel bright and airy.
↓

Custom radiator covers can make new heating units less obtrusive.
↓

the plan

Divvy up a long, rectangular space into distinct grooming areas separated by pocket doors

1 **COMPARTMENTALIZE THE BATH.** Separate chambers for the shower and soaking tub, with separate entrances, add to the feeling of a luxurious, spa-like space.

2 **REWORK THE DRESSING AREA.** To make the bath seem larger, the dressing area was reconfigured to open into the shower room as well as the bedroom.

3 **ADD THE TUB ALCOVE AND WINDOWS.** Expanding 3 feet onto the upper deck required creating an elevated stage and widening a soffit in the kitchen ceiling below to run plumbing.

the details Vintage-look fixtures and fittings capture the style of an 1860s farmhouse

↓**OIL-RUBBED BRONZE** fixtures, including the towel bars, faucet, and tub filler, have a rustic look and provide a welcome visual contrast to the white walls and the other soft tones in the room.

↑**POCKET DOORS** allow for uninterrupted views from one end of the dressing room straight through the window over the tub. The glass shower enclosure and over-the-sink mirrors also capture vistas of the property.

→**NEW WAINSCOTING AND BASEBOARDS** echo the handmade paneling and molding in the home's other bathroom, which is original to the house.

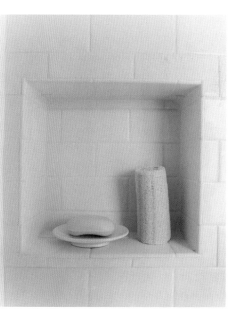

↑**CLEAN WHITE SUBWAY TILE** covers the shower walls, including the niche for toiletries and a built-in bench.

CHAPTER 11

THE COLORFUL BATH

Most of us know the colors we like—we're just afraid to take a chance on putting them up on the wall. Well, on the following pages you'll find plenty of inspiration to help you get over your color phobia. As you'll see, color can do so many things: establish a mood, highlight a room's best features (or camouflage its flaws), brighten up a dark space, or expand a small one. And best of all, a coat of paint is one of the easiest and most affordable upgrades around. So go ahead, be fearless.

THE COLORS OF NATURE— like the real gingko leaves embedded in a resin shower wall, river rocks lining its floor, and sunflower-yellow paint—can make even a basement space like this one feel cheerful and inviting.

IDEA FILE

Whatever your bath-design puzzle, smart use of color can help solve it. Here's a look at just a few of the many things that color can do

↑ CALL ATTENTION TO AN ACCENT. Distressed beadboard paneling, an antique mirror, and a weathered vanity top lend subtle character to a small space, but it's the bold striped fabric that adds eye-catching style.

← LIVEN UP BASIC MATERIALS. Plain white ceramic squares get a cheerful boost from randomly interspersed blue tiles. Mixing the shades of blue visually ties together the bathing and grooming areas, picking up the colors of the laminate vanity top and cabinet knobs.

← **HIGHLIGHT AN ARCHITECTURAL FEATURE.**
White woodwork pops off colored walls. Rooms with
wainscot naturally lend themselves to a two-color
treatment. Opposites on the color wheel, like the
yellow and violet here, make striking combinations.
Called complementary colors, they enhance each
other's energy; pairing colors of similar intensity
keeps the effect in balance.

↑ **STAND UP TO BRIGHT LIGHT.**
Vibrant colors work well where
there's an abundance of natural
light, which could make more
subdued hues appear washed out.

↑ **CREATE A FOCAL POINT.** You don't need
bold colors to achieve a dramatic effect. Neutrals
with attitude—dark taupe, paper-bag brown, dark
khaki, grayed greens, and soft yellows, like the
shades in this tile—can do the job just as well.

→ **AMP UP A DARK SPACE.** A colorful "show wall" adds drama and brightness to a small, windowless bath. Before they settled on a color combination, the homeowners experimented with different tile patterns glued on pieces of wallboard. Zingy colors like these look most at home in contemporary settings.

→ ADD DRAMA TO A PLAIN SPACE. Singling out one surface for color—like this vibrant blue floor—is an easy way to liven up a space. It provides a sharp contrast to the crisp white walls and picks up on the watery hues of the hand-decorated tub.

← CREATE A COZY FEELING. Lining the tub area with blue subway tile creates a distinct niche within the bath. Continuing the tile on the ceiling adds to the sense of enclosure. As a rule, darker colors lower ceilings visually (which is why most people paint their ceilings white), but in some situations, color on the ceiling adds comfort and personality.

✴ DESIGN ADVICE
Cool colors—blues, greens, and clean whites—are perceived as restful and soothing, ideal for creating a sense of calm in a private room like the bath.

→ **MODERNIZE AN OLD SPACE.** A pop of nontraditional color, like the shocking pink on these walls, puts a contemporary spin on traditional styling and gives a whole new look to the beadboard walls and weathered wide-plank floors.

DESIGN ADVICE

Neighbors on the color wheel, like the soft yellow and pale green seen here, create a harmonious effect when paired. Opposites on the wheel deliver a more vibrant punch.

↑ **MAKE A SMALL SPACE FEEL BIGGER.** You'd think that big, fat stripes would dwarf a small bath. In fact, the opposite is true. Wide horizontal stripes "push out" the walls, expanding the space. The trick is to layer soft, related shades, without too much contrast, so that the eye is drawn sideways.

→ **TRANSFORM A ROOM ON THE CHEAP.** A fresh coat of paint is still the fastest, easiest, and most affordable way to refresh a room. If you think a strong color will overwhelm your space, restrict it to just one wall or two.

↓ **ACCENTUATE TRIM AND MOLDINGS.** Darker colors emphasize shadow lines in the paneling, whereas white paint has a reflective quality that tends to blend details. The abundance of blue also makes the bath feel cozy, appropriate for the snug, nautically inspired space.

Choosing and using color

If you freeze in the aisle of paint strips at the home center, you're not alone. Here are some pro tips for incorporating color successfully.

1 **Test it in different lights.** A paint chip or tile sample is only a guide. To really see how a color will look on your walls, paint a large piece of foam-core board, or mount tiles on a piece of wallboard, then move it around the room for a few days. The quality and amount of natural and artificial light will affect how it looks over the course of the day.

2 **Be aware of color psychology.** Colors evoke an emotional response. In general, cool colors (blues, greens, and clean whites) are perceived as restful and soothing, while warm colors (reds, oranges, and yellows) create a sense of drama and energy. So a space that hits you like a shot of caffeine in the morning may not be conducive to a relaxing nighttime soak. That's why bright colors lend themselves particularly well to powder rooms, where they can provide a "wow" factor in more limited doses.

CHAPTER 12 >
DESIGNING YOUR BATH

Bathrooms today have to do more: accommodate more people, give them more privacy, provide generous storage, and fit luxury amenities such as steam showers and whirlpools. Squeezing it all in is no easy task. But whether the puzzle is a compact powder room, a kid-friendly family bath, or a spa-style master retreat, the approach to solving it always starts the same way. First, consider who will be using the space. Next, think about the number and style of fixtures you'd like. And finally, work out where those fixtures can be placed. While there's usually more than one solution to any bath design challenge, here are some tried-and-true strategies for planning a bathroom that works.

inside

1_ **Master Bath**

2_ **Family Bath**

3_ **Half Bath**

4_ **Extra Bath**

5_ **Accessible Bath**

THREE PLANS FOR A MASTER BATH

A master bath is all about comfort and relaxation. And that requires space: at least 80 square feet for a toilet, sink, shower, and a luxury feature like a whirlpool or soaking tub. Increasingly, master baths are integrated into master suites, which might include a sitting room and walk-in closet or dressing room.

In addition to adding convenience and functionality, those extra spaces help to muffle the sound of water running and cabinets opening and closing, the better to buffer a sleeping person from activity in the bathroom. Because square footage in those layouts is usually abundant, the number and location of fixtures are a matter of personal preference and practical plumbing guidelines.

Where space is tight, the main issue is fitting in all the fixtures. But no matter what the size, the most efficient shared baths take schedules into account. People who get up (and retire) at the same time need a different bathroom design than those who don't.

1 THE BARE MINIMUM When floor space is limited, every inch counts. A pocket door between the sink and bathing/toilet area subdivides without getting in the way. Allow at least a 5-foot run of counter if the sinks share a vanity, or 3 feet for each, plus space between, if they are freestanding.

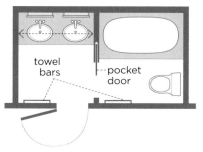

4- to 6-ft.-wide single or double vanity

towel bars

pocket door

2 THE CLASSIC DOUBLED-UP BATH When two people use the bath at the same time every day, the priority is traffic control. Often a "zoned" approach works best, with separate toilet, tub, and shower areas to allow for multiple activities at the same time.

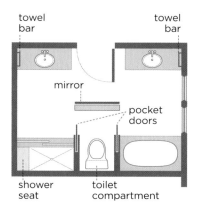

towel bar

towel bar

mirror

pocket doors

shower seat

toilet compartment

3 THE MASTER SUITE BATH If the bath is part of a master suite that also includes a closet or sitting room, take advantage of the extra space to insulate the bedroom from bathroom activity. There can also be a "back door" so that someone can exit the bath without going through the bedroom.

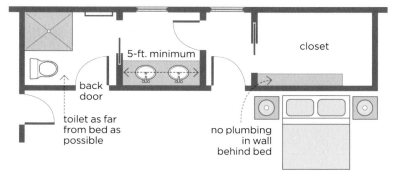

5-ft. minimum

closet

back door

toilet as far from bed as possible

no plumbing in wall behind bed

Creating comfort

Even if you're dealing with a small space, there are a few surefire ways to make any bath more pleasant. **BRIGHTEN IT UP.** As the bathroom expands, so does the need for natural light—the more the better. The best light for a bath comes from above, via skylights or transom/clerestory windows. Higher openings allow better privacy and maximize the effect of light by bouncing it off the ceiling.

AIR IT OUT. Bathrooms are subjected to the most radical microclimate changes of any room in the house. Hot showers increase temperature and humidity to tropical levels, and because the space is shut tight for privacy, steam and odors have no easy way of escaping. Operable windows or skylights help clear the air when the weather is fair, but they need an assist from technology. Consider two exhaust fans—one in the toilet area, the other near the shower.

THE FAMILY BATH: HIGH-TRAFFIC AND KID-FRIENDLY

The family bath is a serious workspace. It's got at least three fixtures (typically toilet, sink, and combination bathtub/shower) and is also the central depository for toothbrushes, towels, medicines, and all manner of grooming gear. The minimum floor space for a three-fixture bathroom is about 40 square feet.

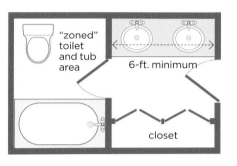

The key to planning a family bath is determining how many people will be using it at the same time. If the whole gang is lining up every morning to get in, consider separating the toilet and shower from the sink area, possibly even in a space with its own entrance that in effect becomes a separate half bath. Or wall off the toilet behind a pocket door, as long as the enclosure is at least 36 inches wide and 66 inches deep. Another option is a stall with half-height walls, which lets in more light and feels less cramped.

Sinks—what type and how many—pose the next question. For a family, double sinks can be handy, but to be really functional they require 6 feet of counter space for everyone and their clutter; anything less and you'll elbow your neighbor while brushing your teeth. As for bathing, remember that regardless of its size, a bathtub needs at least 30 inches of clear floor space for someone to get in and out easily. If you're looking to conserve floor space, a shower stall takes up less than a tub, but choose a stall that is at least 3 feet by 3 feet; anything smaller feels claustrophobic.

Clearances + standard dimensions

For comfort, safety, and accessibility, bathroom fixtures require additional clear floor space, as shown in these industry-recommended minimums. Check building codes for specific clearance requirements in your area.

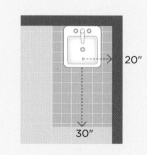

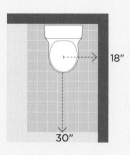

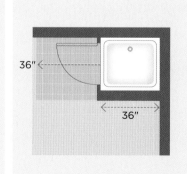

SINK
> 20 inches from center to adjacent wall or fixture
> 30 inches clear space in front

TOILET
> 18 inches from center to adjacent wall or fixture
> 30 inches clear space in front

TUB
> 30 inches clear space from front edge to nearest wall or fixture

SHOWER
> Swinging door requires at least its own width in clear floor space.
> Minimum recommended shower size is 36 by 36 inches.

THE HALF BATH: A SHOWCASE FOR STYLE

With only two fixtures to accommodate, half baths practically design themselves. Minimum dimensions are amazingly compact: You can fit a sink and a toilet into less than 12 square feet and still meet building codes. Half baths don't need much storage, natural light usually is not a priority (a window may even detract from privacy), and less counter space cuts down on clutter.

But there are some practical considerations, starting with the entrance. If possible, the door should swing into the room rather than out, even though that eats up floor space. (A door requires at least its own width in clear floor space to swing open, plus additional room to maneuver so that someone inside the bathroom can shut the door without having to stand on the toilet.) An in-swinging door also avoids the problem of where to "store" the open door. If the space is simply too small, consider a sliding pocket door, which allows you to keep the door open without blocking the hallway.

Fitting in a half bath

If you're thinking about adding a half bath to an existing home, the first task is carving out the space. Here are some planning pointers to get you started.

WHERE TO PUT IT Look for a spot that is easily accessible from the main entertaining areas, but don't put plumbing in a wall shared with the dining or living room, where the added noise would be a nuisance. Consider locating it in the recess under a staircase or converting a large first-floor closet. To save on costs, locate the room adjacent to plumbing lines so that you can tap into the existing water and waste systems.

HOW BIG TO MAKE IT In theory, you could squeeze a sink and toilet into 11 square feet and still meet the International Residential Code. In practice, you'll have enough space if you can find a spot that's about 3 to 4 feet wide and 6 to 8 feet long. Any smaller than that and it won't be comfortable. Going larger is unnecessary, and it's not likely you'll find that much "extra" unused space in your house anyway.

HOW TO LAY IT OUT Traditionally the sink is the focal point, and the toilet is either placed next to it, where it can't be seen when the door's ajar, or on another wall entirely, where it's even less conspicuous. If there's no squeeze on square footage, consider hiding the toilet in a niche created by a half wall, away from the sink basin.

1 TUCKED UNDER A STAIRWAY For privacy's sake, this option works best in homes with an enclosed foyer that opens into adjacent entertaining spaces. The two biggest challenges are providing enough headroom (a minimum of 5 feet above the toilet; check your local codes for height requirements) and ventilation (an exhaust vent will need to be run to the exterior). Place the sink or vanity on the tallest wall so that hand washers won't bump their heads.

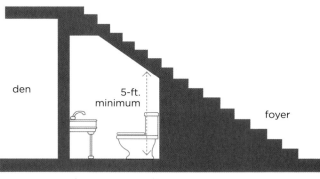

2 CARVED OUT OF A GARAGE This example shows how you can steal space from an attached garage to create a half bath that serves the adjacent kitchen as well as the garage and outdoor areas of the home. Access is via a sliding pocket door, which solves the problem of doors banging into one another or unintended "door traps" that result when they're left open.

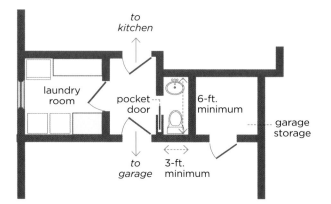

FAMILY POWDER ROOMS

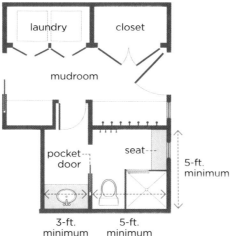

laundry

closet

mudroom

pocket door

seat

5-ft. minimum

3-ft. minimum

5-ft. minimum

The traditional powder room is the architectural equivalent of "good" china or silver—used primarily by visitors on special occasions. But these days, it's being pressed into service as another family bath. After all, potty training needs proximity, dirt is better headed off on the first floor than tracked upstairs, and no one wants to wriggle out of wet workout gear in the bedroom.

Thus evolved the "extra" bath: a half or three-quarters bathroom annexed to a wide variety of household spaces. It can be steps away from the mudroom, garage, or back door; adjacent to a home gym, office, or media room; or off a great-room kitchen.

Designed more for function than for style, a family powder room should focus on materials that are durable, easy to clean, and kid-friendly. If excess dirt is likely, a tile floor with a drain can aid in quick cleanup. Depending on the size and layout of the house, this secondary half bath may include large cabinetry or a linen closet for storing towels and toiletries. It might even act as a miniature pool house when equipped with a small (30-inch) shower, changing area, and a washer/dryer—stretching the limits of the space, not to mention the meaning of the term *powder room* itself.

Outfitting the extra bath

Unlike a powder room that's used primarily by guests, an extra family bath is designed for utility rather than aesthetics. Surfaces need to be durable, easily cleanable, and large enough to accommodate wet towels and dirty laundry.

WAINSCOTING Tongue-and-groove paneling, tile, and solid surfacing can all stand up to abuse. Oil-based semigloss or high-gloss paint and vinyl wall coverings are other tough-wearing options.

LAUNDRY AND TOWEL STORAGE If the room will be used by grubby gardeners or active children, make sure there's a repository for dirty clothes and wet towels, and sufficient shelf space for a supply of fresh towels.

DRYING SPACE It's a good idea to incorporate a pull-out clothesline in the shower for drying damp clothes, hand-washed items, or other wet garments.

FLOOR DRAINS While stone and tile floors are easily cleaned, adding an integral floor drain makes it possible to literally hose down the premises if the bath gets grimy.

BATH OF THE FUTURE

Whether you're building a bath from scratch or remodeling an existing one, it may make sense to incorporate "universal" design features. Intended to make a space easier for someone with physical limitations to use, the principles of accessible design comply with standards established by the Americans with Disabilities Act (ADA). Thinking about accessibility now can yield dividends down the line, allowing you (or an elderly relative) to live comfortably at home even as your physical needs change.

ACCESSIBLE DESIGN GUIDELINES
The National Kitchen and Bath Association (nkba.org) provides guidelines for making a bath more functional for people of all ages, sizes, and abilities. Here are a few of its recommendations. (Other state and local codes may apply.)
> Use slip-resistant surfaces for flooring, as well as for tub and shower bottoms.
> Make doorways at least 32 inches wide to accommodate wheelchairs. (1)
> Provide clear floor space at least 60 inches in diameter, enough for a wheelchair to turn around. (2)
> Give countertop surfaces rounded, radiused, or clipped edges. (3)
> Place shower controls 38 to 48 inches above the floor, low enough to be reached by seated bathers as well as children. (4)

> Include hand sprayers for showers and tubs.
> Make sure showers have a pressure-balancing valve to prevent hot or cold water surges.
> Choose easily operated lever-type faucet handles and bathtub controls. (5)
> Set grab bars 33 to 36 inches off the floor. (6)
> Install shower seats that are at least 15 inches deep and 17 to 19 inches above the floor. (7)

CHAPTER 12 >
FIXTURES + FITTINGS

Tub, sink, shower, toilet. Seems so basic. But each element of the bath demands choices. Freestanding tub or built-in? Pedestal sink or console? One flush or two? And showers—well, the possibilities for customization there are nearly limitless. The following pages will give you a head start on choosing the fixtures and fittings that work best for your style and space. But no matter how simple or lavish your design scheme, if you invest in quality fixtures and arrange them with an eye toward comfort and practicality, you'll enjoy the results for years to come.

inside

>SINKS

ONCE, A BATHROOM SINK WAS JUST A SINK. Today it's a glass vessel, or a hammered-copper basin, or a floating piece of sculpture that our grandparents wouldn't recognize as a sink at all. While the dizzying variety can make choosing one a challenge, it also means there's an option to suit every need, taste, and budget.

In addition to being stylish enough to serve as a focal point of the bath, many of today's lavs are also problem-solvers, shaped and scaled to suit the space you have to work with, no matter how big, small, awkward, or short on storage. While manufacturers offer suites of fixtures, don't think you have to choose the model they market along with your tub or toilet. Feel free to mix and match. In the end, base your decision on the appropriate combination of style and material.

styles

Lavs today rival any other design element in the bath

→**VESSEL** As much a showpiece as a sink, an above-the-counter basin is designed to attract attention. You can mount one on virtually any surface, but a more water-resistant deck is better, as it is likely to get hit with splashes.

→**PEDESTAL** Great where space is tight, a pedestal takes up less room than a vanity or console, and the graceful lines add a touch of class to any bath. The downside is limited storage and deck space. Plumbing is partially (though not entirely) hidden behind the base.

→**CONSOLE** A console typically offers more landing space for toiletries than a pedestal, and many models have extra towel bars on the sides. The classic is a chrome-legged stand with marble top and undermount sink, but you can also get them with vitreous china tops or vary the look by choosing a different finish for the legs.

MOUNTING OPTIONS

Drop-in

The easiest type of sink to install, these simply drop into a hole cut into the countertop. The sink's rim supports its weight; caulking around the perimeter keeps the seal watertight. Also called self-rimming sinks, these can work with just about any countertop material. The downside is that dirt can collect around the exposed rim.

Undermount

These attach with clips to the underside of the countertop. The look is sleek and seamless, and it's easy to keep the counter surface clean. But because undermounts leave the edge of the countertop exposed to water, they can only be used with certain materials, chiefly stone and solid surfacing.

Wall-mount

These have the advantage of being adjustable to almost any height, making them ideal for handicapped or children's baths. And because wall-mounts don't require a cabinet for support, they're often the best option where floor space is limited. Some models come with a "shroud" to cover the exposed plumbing, or you can get a decorative P-trap to match your hardware.

Integral

With an integral sink, the basin and countertop are one continuous material, typically solid surfacing, metal, stone, or concrete. You can drop one of these onto a vanity, set it atop a console, or mount it directly on the wall. Because there are no seams anywhere, they're the best option for neat freaks.

Above-mount

Like an old-fashioned washbasin, a vessel sink sits atop the counter. If you want one, you have to plan for it well in advance: The vanity may need to be lower than normal to make up for the raised sink height, and faucets must be mounted on the wall or the surround. Because the bowl is completely exposed, it's more vulnerable to damage and may not be the most practical choice for some baths.

Materials

VITREOUS CHINA is durable, affordable, and the standard for fine bath fixtures. Made by firing ceramic clay at high temperatures to form a glasslike, nonporous surface, it's easy to clean and doesn't require special care. Vitreous china sinks are available in colors, but white is the perennial favorite. $$

FIRECLAY is a tough ceramic commonly used for European farmhouse sinks. Highly resistant to chipping and scratching, it's often chosen for lavs with a handcrafted look. $$

PORCELAIN ENAMEL, essentially a glasslike coating bonded to a metal base, is another classic choice for durability, affordability, and glossy good looks. Traditionally, such sinks were porcelain enamel over cast iron; today, the metal is as likely to be lighter-weight steel. $-$$

SOLID SURFACING lends itself to integral basins, where the sink and countertop are a seamless unit. The acrylic is impervious to just about anything in a bath (water, soap, steam, scratches, stains), comes in dozens of colors and patterns, and can look like marble, granite, concrete, or, well, plastic. $$

STONE can also be used for integral sinks, but it's best suited for vessels, which show off its natural beauty. Because stone is heavy, some undermount and wall-mounted models require additional support. Cultured stone is a lighter and less expensive imitator, made from crushed stone and resins. $$-$$$

CONCRETE delivers the heft of stone at a lower cost. It can be molded into virtually any shape and tinted nearly any color, with striking results. Most often used for integral sinks and countertops, it needs regular resealing to stay water-resistant. $$-$$$

GLASS is more durable than it looks. It's usually molded into vessels with 1-inch-thick walls and tempered so it won't shatter, but you may want to avoid putting one where items can fall on it. $$-$$$

WOOD sinks are among the most expensive, because their construction is so intricate. The wood's natural resins (typical species are iroko, teak, and maple) are extracted and replaced with artificial resins; then the wood is sealed with lacquer or polyurethane to prevent moisture absorption. $$-$$$

METAL, a kitchen staple, has moved into the bath. In addition to stainless steel, options include bronze, copper, nickel, even gold-plated brass. Some finishes develop a patina (unless you want to polish). $$

>FAUCETS

NOTHING ADDS CHARACTER to a bathroom like a classic two-handle faucet with porcelain Hot and Cold buttons and an elegant shepherd's-crook spout. No, wait. Maybe nothing adds character like a streamlined wall-mount spigot with a single-handle control. Or a graceful gooseneck with lever handles. Or—well, you get the point; there are so many faucet styles out there that you can give a room a new look in the time it takes to swap out a spigot.

One thing holds true regardless of your taste or budget: You should spring for rugged, solid-brass construction and a drip-proof ceramic disc valve. After dropping a fairly hefty chunk of change on your new faucet, you want to enjoy what's distinctive about it without worrying about function.

WALL-MOUNTS can be any style, like these sleekly elegant cross handles and spout, but require more planning than a standard installation because the plumbing has to be set at exactly the right height before the walls can be finished.

FINISHES

Most faucets are made of brass, a durable, easily cast metal that polishes to a beautiful golden shine. Left to its own devices, though, that shine quickly tarnishes to a rough brownish-green. Clear coats of lacquer will keep brass bright, at least until the delicate finish gets nicked or scratched.

For longer-lasting, maintenance-free protection, manufacturers electroplate brass with thin layers of corrosion-resistant metals, including chrome, nickel, platinum, gold—whatever the budget can bear. The most durable faucet finishes are applied using a process called physical vapor deposition, or PVD, which uses a vacuum chamber to bond the coating to the underlying surface. The result can look like polished brass, bronze, nickel, or pewter, yet is nearly invulnerable to scratching or corrosion. Contrast that with so-called "living" finishes, such as weathered brass and copper, which are meant to darken and develop a patina as they age.

styles

There's a faucet to fit every type of sink and any kind of setup

→ **SINGLE HOLE** These take up the least amount of deck space. Spout and handles emerge from the same stem, so only one hole is needed in the countertop. Many single-hole styles have one handle that controls both hot and cold water, but you can also get them in more traditional two-handle versions.

↓ **MINI WIDESPREAD** Scaled-down versions of standard widespread faucets, these are great if you want a traditional look but don't have the space—say, in a small powder room. They fit in as few as 4 inches and don't have the escutcheon plate that connects a centerset's spout and handles.

← **CENTERSET** Like single-hole models, centerset faucets are space-savers (also money-savers, as these are generally the least expensive type of faucets). Holes for the hot and cold supplies are typically 4 inches apart, with the handles and spout clustered together on a common base.

↑ **BRIDGE** Developed in the late 19th century as a way to connect hot and cold water supplies at a single tap, these look great in a period bath, but the raised spout also makes them a practical choice with modern vessel sinks, which sit higher on the countertop.

↑ **WIDESPREAD** The most popular and versatile of faucet styles, these require three holes in the countertop: one for each handle and one for the spout. The outermost holes are typically 8 inches apart on center, though the span can be as few as 6 or as many as 12 inches.

>TUBS

TODAY'S TUBS make getting clean almost an afterthought. Deep soaking pools, muscle-massaging water jets, softly soothing air bubbles—you can get just about any feature you want in a style and size that will suit your decor. Ditto for materials. Worried about hauling that heavy enameled cast-iron claw-foot up the stairs? You can find the same style in a lighter (and less expensive) acrylic or porcelain-coated steel.

When deciding which tub to buy, think first about the look you want to achieve. If you're going for period authenticity, match the tub to the style and age of the house. For a more eclectic look, play different styles off each other. Bring along your bathroom dimensions as well as measurements for an existing tub recess or niche. A standard tub is 60 inches long, 30 inches wide, and about 16 inches deep, but you can get them longer, wider, and deeper. And before you commit, make sure to hop in and see how it feels.

↑FREESTANDING
If you've got the space, a freestanding tub becomes a natural focal point in the bath. Claw-foot tubs remain the go-to choice for vintage style, but other popular options include slipper (a claw-foot variation with one or two raised ends), pedestal, or skirted styles.

styles

With tub options in so many different shapes and sizes, it's easy to get into hot water

← SOAKING Often in sculptural styles and exotic materials, soaking tubs are all about relaxing. Most are larger and deeper than conventional drop-in models, like this reproduction of a 1930s-era soaker, which is an expansive 70 inches long and 25 inches high.

← WHIRLPOOL These acrylic tubs come in a wide variety of shapes and sizes. Because they have motorized components that need to be hidden, they're usually dropped into a surround, although it's possible these days to find freestanding models, even some with traditional styling.

↓ DROP-IN Tubs that fit into a surround can be customized for any bath. Drop-in tubs, which have no finished sides, can be under-mounted or, like this one, can have a lip that sits on the tub deck.

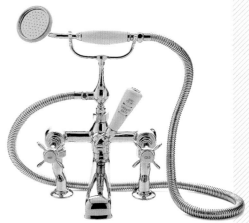

TUB SPOUTS + FILLERS

Like lav faucets, tub fillers can be deck mounted or wall mounted; they can also be freestanding. Clean-looking wall-mounted faucets or deck-mounts are standard for tubs that drop into a surround. Tubs that sit away from the wall require freestanding fillers, with plumbing lines run under the floor.

No matter which style of tub filler you choose, think about placement. If you're going to lean back and soak, position the faucet in the middle of the tub or angle it in such a way that it won't interfere with bathing. Whatever style you settle on, make sure it has brass components and ceramic disc valves.

The surest way to ruin a bathing experience is not having enough hot water. A large-capacity tub may require that you install a larger water heater or a tankless model that can provide a steady supply.

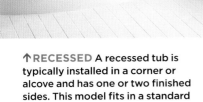

↑ RECESSED A recessed tub is typically installed in a corner or alcove and has one or two finished sides. This model fits in a standard 5-foot niche, but its curved apron creates a more generous interior.

>SHOWERS

AAH, THE REJUVENATING EFFECT of a hot shower. Modern shower fittings can deliver a drenching soak, even while adhering to water-saving requirements. Of course, you can also up the ante (and the water consumption) with rainheads the size of dinner plates, multiple body sprays, waterfall spigots, and steam-generating nozzles. Just make sure your water heater is brawny enough: Because multijet systems pump out 10 to 30 gallons per minute, you'll need an 80- to 100-gallon water heater (versus the standard 40) if you plan to take long showers. You may also need to replace ½-inch supply lines with ¾-inch or 1-inch pipe to handle the volume of water at the pressure that's required.

→ CUSTOM
MULTIJET
SHOWER
At the highest end of the spectrum in cost and complexity, custom showers can deliver a head-to-toe sensory experience. This one does it with a fixed showerhead, an adjustable hand shower, and a pair of body sprays.

Nothing beats the custom-shower experience, but modular and retrofit units can come pretty close

→ **SHOWER COLUMN** If you want to upgrade your shower without tearing open the walls, these prefab units have multiple water features already built in, delivering the custom-shower experience with easier installation and less expense. Simply connect the preplumbed panel to your existing hot and cold water lines, and blast away.

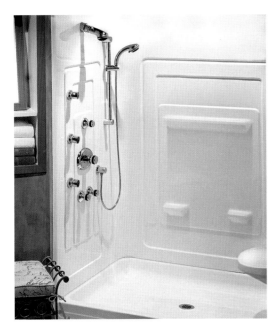

↑**SHOWER MODULE** Whole-stall systems are perhaps the easiest way to get a luxury shower experience. Everything is included in the acrylic shell: multiple body jets, storage niches, built-in seating, even a steam generator, though the space-capsule look of such a unit might be out of place in an elegant master bath.

↑**STEAM SHOWER** With the touch of a button, a breadbox-size steam generator hidden outside the shower sends soothing clouds of vapor through a steam head in the stall. It doesn't use much water—a 20-minute steam consumes a mere 2 gallons—but requires electricity and some extra labor to make the shower stall (and the entire bath) steamproof.

SHOWERHEADS

CEILING-MOUNT
These large-diameter fixtures, mounted directly overhead, offer a better drenching than a standard spray head. If you don't always want a head-to-toe soaking, though, you'll also need a handheld spray or body jets.

WALL-MOUNT Upgrading your shower is as easy as twisting a new low-flow showerhead on the existing shower arm.

HANDHELD The trend in today's bath is customization, and that extends to the shower fittings. A variable-height handheld spray is often installed along with a fixed shower-head, especially in shared baths.

>TOILETS

WHILE TOILETS WILL never be the stars of the bath, an ever-greater range of designs and innovative new technologies have brought them out of the shadows. Much of the change is thanks to increasingly tight water restrictions, which have forced manufacturers to come up with ways to improve functionality. On the style front, you can find a toilet to complement just about any kind of decor, with options from historic reproductions to models so futuristic you can't even find the tank.

Regardless of their appearance, most toilets are either gravity operated or pressure assisted. Where water pressure is low, gravity flush is the way to go. Where house-to-sewer drains are long or prone to clogging, the extra oomph of a pressure tank can help.

The best toilets have 3-inch-diameter flush valves and wide, fully glazed trapways. Beyond that, the choice comes down to what best fits your space, taste, and budget.

→ TWO-PIECE The classic toilet has a separate tank and bowl made of vitreous china. A straight-skirted base like this one is easier to keep clean than one that reflects the curves of the trapway.

styles

Today's toilets offer good looks, easy care, and water savings

← WALL-MOUNT To conserve space, keep floor area open, or create a more modern look, toilets can hang on the wall, with the tank recessed between the studs. The flush actuator is above or beside the bowl on a panel that also provides access to the tank. Wall-mounts are great in a handicap-accessible bath, because the bowl can be hung at a comfortable height for the user.

→ ONE-PIECE These are typically lower in profile and more contemporary in styling than two-piece models. They also have some functional advantages: The low tank allows for additional shelf space above, and they're easy to clean because the transition area between tank and bowl is a single, wipeable surface.

↑ DUAL-FLUSH To save on water consumption, these offer two different flush options: a standard 1.6-gallon flush, and a 0.8-gallon flush for liquid-only waste. Some new models, called high-efficiency toilets, use even less water.

↑ SPECIALTY If you really want to, you can get a toilet with a heated or lighted seat, built-in fans, washing and drying functions, even sound effects. All you need is an electrical connection and plenty of cash.

BIDETS

If you have the space, you might want to consider including a bidet in your design. Typically the bidet is installed next to the toilet, but if it's only going to be used by the female half of a couple, it may make more sense for traffic control to put it in "her" part of a shared bath.

A bidet occupies the same amount of floor space as a toilet—about 30 inches. If the bidet and toilet will be side by side, allow at least 15 inches in between. In addition to running a drain line and supplies for both hot and cold water, you may want to accommodate a few extras for convenience: a soap holder, a towel bar, and a hook for hanging clothing.

>LIGHTING

WHEN IT COMES TO interior lighting, bathrooms are probably given the least consideration of all the rooms in the house. That's a shame. Done right, bath lighting can give a boost to the start of your day or help you unwind in the evening.

A good bathroom lighting plan is a series of layers, directing illumination where it's needed for showering, shaving, or putting on makeup, while ambient sources enhance the overall mood of the room. Positioning the fixtures correctly is the first step. Equally important is the quality of light itself. The crisp white light of halogen bulbs tends to render skin tones most accurately, but new compact fluorescent bulbs also offer good color rendering while they save you money on energy usage.

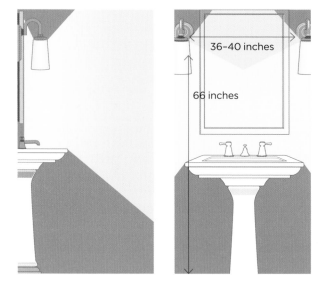

36–40 inches

66 inches

LIGHTING THE VANITY RIGHT

The most common mistake people make is putting recessed ceiling fixtures directly over the mirror. An overhead light shining on top of your head will create shadows under your eyes, chin, and nose, making you look tired. The best way to create even illumination in front of a bathroom mirror is through cross lighting, with fixtures at eye level on either side of the mirror. That way, both halves of the face are lit equally, without unflattering shadows. (Fixtures can be mounted directly on the mirror if it's large.) For best results, fixtures should be 36 to 40 inches apart and about 66 inches above the floor. If the light has to be mounted over the vanity, it should be 75 to 80 inches above the floor and at least 24 inches long. At minimum, vanity lighting should deliver 150 watts of illumination.

styles

Ideally, a bath should have at least three different types of illumination

→ **TASK LIGHTING**
Vanity lighting gets top consideration for shaving and applying makeup. Fixtures on either side of the mirror cast the most even light. Wall-mounted sconces are the most popular, but there's no reason you can't use hanging pendants, as long as they don't get in the way when you're standing at the vanity.

→ **NATURAL LIGHT**
Nothing works better than daylight for making the bath a pleasant space. Skylights in particular are great because they let you see out without letting others see in. Over the tub is an ideal spot, inviting a view of the outdoors while you bathe. Operable windows and skylights also improve bathroom ventilation.

→ **AMBIENT LIGHTING**
This "fill-in" light provides general (as opposed to task) illumination. There are lots of ways to get more creative with ambient lighting than a flush-mount ceiling fixture. You could go with a chandelier, track lighting, or cove lighting—rope lights tucked behind a molding or under a toekick— which adds a soft glow around the perimeter of the room or in a tub alcove. A toekick light can also function as a great night-light.

↑**ACCENT LIGHTING** A small spotlight directed at a piece of art or a beautiful wall treatment creates another layer of illumination in the bathroom. Similarly, a recessed ceiling fixture can be angled to highlight tilework or fixtures and make them sparkle.

>ACCESSORIES

IF YOU DON'T WANT TO SPRING FOR A SPA-STYLE TUB or custom-built steam shower, you can still add panache and personality with affordable accessories. Streamlined or sculptural, vintage or contemporary, in antique bronze or gleaming chrome, there's a suite of hardware that's right for your space. And you don't have to stop at coordinating your towel rack with your toilet-paper holder; bath accoutrements are increasingly offered as part of collections that also include faucets, showerheads, even toilet-tank levers.

1   COORDINATED FLUSHERS Instead of settling for the toilet maker's tank lever, you can swap it out for one that complements your Victorian-style powder room or modern master bath.

2   HALF CIRCLE An open ring makes towel draping easy. This dark finish—oil-rubbed bronze with copper highlights—would look great against a light travertine tile background.

3   DOUBLE DUTY Swing-out racks are a sleek space saver in small baths. The swiveling arms are also great for drying delicate hand washables.

4   BATHROOM BLING Crystal accents give this nautical-style double robe hook a little flash—the perfect compromise for a his-and-hers bath.

5   GREEN RINGS Bamboo-inspired towel rings bring a bit of Zen into your bath. Like the plant itself, these are environmentally friendly, cast from lead-free pewter.

6   UNHINGED For a rustic cottage or farmhouse bath, simple, unembellished wrought iron fits in nicely. This paper holder, modeled on carriage-house hardware, has a vintage feel.

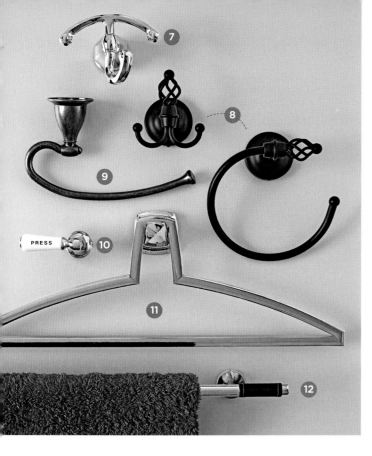

7 QUICK HOOKUP The lower arm of this double-duty robe hook swivels, making it easy to hang multiple items.

8 CLASSIC BLACK Design pros point to darker finishes as a hot bathroom trend. The twisted birdcage finials on these black, powder-coated zinc accessories look at home in anything from a country cottage bath to a neoclassical retreat.

9 MINI BAR If you lack the wall space for a full-size rod but prefer its ease of use to a hook or ring, new 8-inch bars offer the best of both worlds. Perfect for that powder-room hand towel.

10 VINTAGE FLUSHER Complete your period bath with a reproduction brass-and-porcelain lever that can retrofit onto most modern toilet tanks.

11 ROBE VALET An old-fashioned concept turned modern, this polished-chrome robe hanger makes a distinctive silhouette on a master bathroom wall.

12 A TOUCH OF LEATHER Flashes of color and texture, like the stitched leather wrapping the ends of this simple, thin rod, pump up the personality of plain fixtures.

TOWEL WARMERS

Towel warmers do more than just toast your terry. They also help control mildew in damp areas, provide a supplemental heat source in cold climates, and dry unmentionables with ease.

These floor- or wall-mounted units come in two basic types, electric and hydronic. The former gets hardwired or simply plugged in; warm oil circulating inside the rails provides the heat. Hydronic units, which work more like radiators, are plumbed directly into a house's existing hot-water system.

If you're worried about bumping into one in the altogether, most towel warmers will turn off after reaching 150 degrees—too hot to hold on to, but not hot enough to pose a real danger.

1 TOWER
A basket-type unit is sculptural and functional: The more tightly bunched the towel, the more thoroughly it warms.

2 CORNER
Where space is tight, a curved-bar heater can squeeze into a corner.

3 PIVOTING
A hinged rack can hug the wall or swing out to create a partition.

4 FREESTANDING
A plug-in unit with an internal heating element goes anywhere you want it—say, poolside to warm robes.

CHAPTER 14

MATERIALS + FINISHES

Since a bathroom has to meet so many demands, what you put on the walls, floors, and countertops can make or break your enjoyment of a bath remodel. The choice depends not just on your style and budget, but also on how well a material stands up to daily use and how much maintenance it requires. On the upside, there's more than enough variety out there for you to find appropriate selections in every style and at every price point. The real challenge is narrowing down the choices. Here's a rundown of pros, cons, and considerations.

inside

1_ **Walls + Floors**
glass, ceramic, stone, wood, great combos

2_ **Choices for Vanity Tops**
stone, solid surfacing, concrete, laminate, glass and composite

>WALLS + FLOORS

BATHROOM SURFACES have to meet very specific requirements, chiefly that they stand up to water, clean up easily, and, in the case of flooring, be safe underfoot.

The materials that show up most often in the bath—stone, ceramic, porcelain, glass, and wood—can be used on both vertical and horizontal surfaces. Running the flooring material up the walls creates a seamless look that works well in a small bath. But mixing and matching can yield dramatic results, too, as you'll see from the examples on these pages.

Flooring is generally installed before cabinetry, so bear in mind that it will need to be protected while the rest of your project is completed.

MARBLE TILES on the floor and skinny white bricks on the wall maximize reflected light in a bath that lacks windows. The high-gloss finishes suit the setting, a former industrial loft.

GLASS TILE

Glass tile comes subtly or brilliantly colored; clear, iridescent, or matte; molded into shapes or textured into designs; even tumbled into nuggets like pebbles at the seashore. And when you use it to line a shower stall or add depth to a floor, you're not only ratcheting up the style quotient in your house, you're also making landfills a little lighter; some of the best-selling products are made from recycled wine bottles and window glass.

Once grouted into place, glass makes a rugged surface underfoot. It's also easy to care for—cleanup requires only mild soap and water—and doesn't need sealing. Keep in mind that the smaller the tile, the safer the surface, since tiles are surrounded by more skid-resistant grout. Tumbled-glass tiles, which are softer in feel and appearance than transparent ones, are also less slippery. **$$–$$$**

← **TRANSPARENT GLASS** has a watery look that's perfect in the bath. With its big window and double skylights, this glass-tiled enclosure feels almost like an outdoor shower—a fitting choice since it's on a houseboat. Mixing different shapes and sizes of the same tile creates a pleasing pattern.

→ **MOSAIC TILES** with a copper-colored glass backing make for a rich-looking floor. The colors pass through $\frac{3}{16}$ inch of clear glass, giving the surface a depth and gloss not possible with any other material.

PORCELAIN TILE

THE STRONGEST TYPE OF CERAMIC TILE, porcelain is made of dry, powdered clay pressed into shape and fired at an extremely high temperature. The resulting tile is nonporous, resistant to staining and scratching, and easy to keep clean. Unglazed porcelain tiles are slip-resistant and color-through, so they won't show wear. Glazed porcelain tiles come in a huge array of colors and styles. Most porcelain tiles mimic natural stone but without stone's vulnerabilities or maintenance needs. **$–$$**

CERAMIC TILE

Molded from red or white clay, glazed with color, then baked, ceramic tile comes in a dazzling array of patterns, hues, and textures. With so many options available at so many price points, you might want to take a mix-and-match approach: Alternate colors, insert decorative tiles into plain fields, or add ornamental borders. Creatively placed, handmade artisanal tiles can turn an ordinary wall into an affordable design statement.

Ceramic tile is durable and waterproof, though the grout between tiles must be sealed periodically. Handmade tile tends to be more fragile than machine-made (also more expensive). Matte finishes, glazes that contain sand, and embossed designs add traction. **$–$$**

top pick

WALL TREATMENT: SUBWAY TILE

For the classic turn-of-the-century bath, the material of choice is subway tile. The name comes from the wall covering in New York City's underground transit stations, which opened in 1904. Its popularity means you can find subway tile in a wide variety of materials, sizes, and glazes: ceramic, porcelain, or glass; small rectangles or large; square or beveled edges; matte or high-gloss sheen. At the lowest end of the price scale are machine-made ceramic tiles with a uniform ¼-inch thickness. Higher-end handmade versions are thicker but less consistent. The variations add visual interest but make them trickier to install.

BEVEL-EDGED subway tile (left) in glossy white looks clean and catches the light. Square-edged tile (above) is more traditional; with an antique finish, it takes on a softer appearance.

STONE

Natural stone has plenty going for it as a design element in the bath. Each piece emerges from the earth with its own distinctive color and pattern, which means there's a type of stone to suit just about any bathroom scheme. It's impervious to water (though most varieties need sealing) and will last as long as your house does. Perhaps the only thing that doesn't work in stone's favor is the price; relative to most other materials, it's expensive, owing to the high cost of quarrying, shipping, and fabricating. $$–$$$

↓POPULAR OPTIONS for the bath include (from top) granite, honed marble, slate, limestone, polished marble, and travertine.

↑CLEFT SLATE, with its distinctive surface texture and earthy color variations, brings a touch of warmth and softness to the walls of a masculine bath. Green-flecked Jura limestone, honed to a smooth finish, tops the vanity.

←**TRAVERTINE** gets its distinctive pockmarked finish from water that percolated through the stone as it formed. The tumbled tiles give this open shower a soft, antique look, enhanced by the oil-rubbed finish on the hardware.

↑**MARBLE** remains the material of choice for a classic bath. Here it's used in multiple ways: a richly veined slab covering the vanity and forming the backsplash, 1-inch tiles on the floor, and larger tiles lining the shower stall.

→**LIMESTONE SLABS,** ½ inch thick, show off the material's dramatic veining in a way that smaller tiles can't. This stone comes from France, though limestone is quarried all over the world.

WALLS AND FLOORS:
MOSAIC PATTERNS

While you may think of mosaic tiles as itty-bitty squares that create a pattern or picture, the term can apply to tiles as large as 2 by 2 inches. Mosaic tile can be made from clay, glass, metal, or even wood, but the favored material, especially for the bath, is marble. Use mosaics to add color, pattern, and texture to walls, floors, and backsplashes. Because complicated designs require laborious handwork—a square foot can contain hundreds of tesserae, as the tiny tiles are called—such mosaics can be extremely expensive, topping out at hundreds of dollars per square foot. To keep costs down, use mosaics as borders or insets surrounded by less costly field tiles, or stick to an allover pattern instead of a custom picture or design.

Mosaics come already mounted on mesh backing, so installers don't have to labor over spacing lots of little pieces. Still, you'll want an experienced tile setter for intricate designs. Once in place, a mosaic is unaffected by humidity or water.

↓ **A MOSAIC BORDER** can lend interest to a plain floor, help define a room, or add classic style. It's also a way to incorporate a fancy material at moderate cost.

↑ **AN ALLOVER PATTERN** of tiny glass mosaic tiles turns a shower stall into an eye-catching centerpiece in the bath. The tiles come premounted on 12-by-12-inch sheets for easy installation; the homeowners did most of this job themselves.

→ **AN INSET** turns the tub surround into an instant focal point. Its colors and pattern reference mosaic tilework's Mediterranean roots and look right at home in the Spanish Eclectic–style house.

WOOD

For years, people have been skittish about using wood in the bathroom, where puddles are inevitable and humidity levels notoriously high. Nowadays, however, thanks to better ventilation, the preference for separate shower stalls, and improved finishes that resist water, the bath is a more wood-friendly environment than ever before.

A favorite for vanities and accent trim, wood is showing up more frequently on walls, floors, and tub surrounds. Stained or left natural, it warms up a space that can sometimes feel cold. Painted, it's just the thing for the relaxed look of a seaside or cottage-style bath.

You still need to be vigilant, of course, and take care to towel up splashes promptly, but these days there's a lot less to worry about when using wood in the bath. **$–$$$**

↓**SOME HARDWOODS,** including oak, cherry, and maple, are naturally resistant to moisture. But the wet feet, drips, and soggy towels of a busy bathroom tax even the most stable boards, so you may want to think twice before installing wood if maintenance would pose problems.

↑**NATURAL CHERRY** is the star of this bath, used for paneling, trim, cabinets, and even inlays on the radiant-heated tile floor. A hand-rubbed finish makes the wood shimmer, as if it were burnished by years of use.

← **THE WOOD TUB SURROUND** and multicolored slate floor make this bath inviting. When using wood on a tub deck, it's important to seal any exposed grain, such as around the faucet holes, and to run a bead of caulk around the tub's lip to keep water from infiltrating.

↑ **WOOD FLOORING** stained a rich brown looks dramatic in an otherwise neutral-colored bath. In the tub area, wood requires extra attention to drips and splashes, proper sealing, and careful installation to make sure there are no gaps where water can get underneath.

← **PAINTED PANELING** gives a dreamy look to an all-white cottage bath. Wood lines the wall two ways: beadboard on the lower portion, horizontal panels above. Mixing up the treatments assures that the material won't look boring.

↘ PAINTED BEADBOARD is the classic wall covering for informal spaces like bathrooms and hallways. Unlike more formal wainscot styles, it's also good in small spaces, where you don't have to get far away to appreciate it.

→ FLAT-PANEL WAINSCOT, used here on the walls and tub surround, has a more formal look than beadboard. Its simple, clean lines give this traditionally styled bath (the "hers" half of a his-and-hers setup) a spare elegance. The same wall treatment is used in the husband's bath, too, tying the two spaces together visually.

top pick

WALLS:
WAINSCOT

Wood wainscot is traditional, but there are several newfangled ways to get the look. Planks made of medium-density fiberboard (MDF) are milled to look like high-end painted beadboard but won't expand, contract, or warp in a damp environment—provided you use MDF specially treated to withstand moisture. Wide sheets of MDF or solid surfacing cover walls quickly with few or no gaps and, in the case of solid surfacing, no concerns about moisture.

↑ CERAMIC TILE "BEADBOARD" is inspired by the real thing but sheds water, making it a smart choice for a jetted tub surround.

great combos MIX-AND-MATCH MATERIALS

With so many great materials to choose from—and new ones being introduced all the time—it's hard to settle on just one. Luckily, you don't have to. Mixing and matching colors, patterns, sizes, and textures can yield beautiful and sometimes surprising results. Here are a few creative approaches to combinations that work.

↓THROW IN SURPRISE ACCENTS. Stainless-steel tiles shimmer alongside recycled glass. Impervious to water, they're a good choice in a shower stall and can also add shine to a backsplash or floor.

←PLAY WITH PATTERN. A random pattern of bamboo and teak mosaic tiles makes an unusual and dramatic wall treatment. Though installed like conventional tile, wood mosaics require special grout that remains flexible as the wood expands and contracts.

←VARY THE PROPORTIONS. Standard-size ceramic subway tile, a border of scaled-down green miniatures, and a skinny liner strip add up to a harmonious combination in a vintage-look bath.

←SHOWCASE A SPECIAL MATERIAL. Used two ways, the same stone gets twice as interesting. Above the border, tumbled limestone mini bricks show off their soft texture. Below, a larger herringbone pattern highlights variations in color.

>CHOICES FOR VANITY TOPS

AS WITH EVERY other surface in the bath, vanity tops offer more options than ever. New technologies have created an explosion of innovative materials, all of them durable, water-resistant, and good-looking. Many of them are green, too, made with recycled and sustainable ingredients.

When it comes to choosing a countertop material, there are a few things to keep in mind. Vanity tops have to be tough enough to stand up to heat and humidity, not to mention soap scum, toothpaste, and makeup. You want something waterproof and easy to clean, of course, but you also need something that's going to work with your chosen sink style. Some materials, such as stone, concrete, and solid surfacing, lend themselves to undermount or integral basins, while others, like laminate, can be used only with drop-in sinks.

→ **ENGINEERED STONE,** also called quartz surfacing, is fabricated and installed like natural stone. It can be cut to any shape and given any edge profile, from an elaborate curved ogee to a simple eased edge, as on this petite vanity top with undermount sink.

NATURAL STONE

Stone makes a statement. And because you need a lot less stone to top a vanity than to cover a kitchen counter, you can make that statement for a lot less dough. Granite, marble, limestone, slate, and soapstone are all tough, handsome, and water-resistant, making them popular bath choices. The harder and less porous the stone, the better it can withstand bathroom spills and scuffs. Softer stone requires more frequent sealing.

There are few limitations to using stone on the vanity—not even cost, as you can often find offcuts from bigger jobs at the stoneyard for a lot less than you'd pay to have a piece fabricated to order. You can also opt for stone tiles instead of slabs, though you'll have to contend with grout lines. **$$–$$$**

← **GRANITE,** owing to its resistance to water, scratching, and staining, makes a great vanity top, especially when you want a stone that polishes to a high shine. Wrapping a piece up the backsplash helps protect the wainscoted wall from water.

→ **MARBLE,** which is softer in both look and composition than granite, needs more frequent sealing and can be vulnerable to the chemicals in certain lotions, cosmetics, and household cleaners. But some people like it better when it's a little weathered, like these Venatino marble surrounds made from stoneyard leftovers.

ENGINEERED STONE

A factory-made mix of 93 percent quartz granules held together with a resin binder, engineered stone combines the ruggedness of granite with the Crayola palette of solid surfacing. It's impervious to chemicals and stains and doesn't need sealing. Man-made stone's predictability means it has none of the natural stuff's vulnerability— but also none of its distinctive veining. You can get it in looks resembling granite, marble, or creamy limestone, or in terrazzo-style blends spiked with mirrored glass or seashells. The cost, less than natural stone, is comparable to that of solid surfacing. **$$**

SOLID SURFACING

A synthetic, nonporous plastic-and-mineral compound that's "renewable" (small scratches and stains can be buffed out), solid surfacing can be given a matte or high-gloss finish. The color palette includes stone look-alikes as well as more whimsical patterns in shades never seen in nature. It's seamless, doesn't need sealing, and shrugs off bathroom chemicals. Solid surfacing is the material most often used for integral sinks, with the basin and countertop in a single piece. **$$**

CONCRETE

Artisans on the West Coast started experimenting with decorative concrete in the 1980s; in the years since, it has evolved into a mainstream alternative to high-end beauty queens like granite and marble. Perhaps the material's biggest draw is its adaptability. In addition to limitless color choices, it can be poured into just about any shape, troweled to any texture, and given any edge profile, so it looks at home in a wide variety of spaces. And because each countertop is handcrafted, it has an artisanal quality that other manufactured materials lack.

Concrete needs regular sealing but otherwise cleans up well with a damp cloth. Because it is fabricated with holes for fixtures, you need to choose your sink and faucet first. For best results, find a concrete craftsman who specializes in kitchens and baths (not driveways), and check out product samples carefully, as no two manufacturers' recipes are identical. **$$–$$$**

PLASTIC LAMINATE

Laminate—plastic bonded to a particleboard substrate—is inexpensive, comes in hundreds of designs, and makes a smooth, easy-to-wipe surface. Price aside, the material owes its enduring popularity to the sheer volume of colors, patterns, and finishes available, from faux stone to wood grain, glossy to matte, even metallics. The downside is that particleboard is vulnerable to water, especially at the seams, so you're limited to self-rimming sinks that cover the edges of the substrate. To get the requisite thickness for a vanity top, you'll need to double up ¾-inch particleboard at the edges to create a 1½-inch face. **$**

GLASS AND COMPOSITE

Glass tile makes a smooth, shimmering surface on countertops and backsplashes as well as walls and floors. If you like a sparkly look, another option is the increasing variety of recycled glass countertops, made from crushed-up bottles (and, in some cases, recycled porcelain) in a cement matrix. Like the terrazzo of old that it imitates, recycled glass surfacing is durable, beautiful, and colorful. It's also a "green" material. Fabricated and installed like stone (and about on par, pricewise), it's manufactured only in slabs, not tiles, so it may not be a practical choice for a small job. **$$–$$$**

CHAPTER 15

STORAGE + BUILT-INS

A place for everything and everything in its place. That's the fantasy of bathroom storage, but we know the truth—cluttered surfaces, crammed drawers, and an under-sink cabinet that barely fits the plumbing pipes. Bath manufacturers feel your pain and offer vanities in every style and size, from petite powder-room stands to furniturelike two-person cabinets. The ultimate, of course, is custom-built storage that captures every available inch of space. We can't make everyone in your family pick up after themselves, but we can give you some clever storage solutions to help get them in the habit.

inside

>VANITY CABINETS

BUYING A READY-MADE vanity doesn't have to be a tradeoff. Manufacturers offer cabinets in every size, style, and configuration, so it's easy to complement your bathroom design scheme while keeping clutter under control.

Like those in the kitchen, bath cabinets come in three basic types. The least costly option is stock cabinetry, which comes in standard widths (from 12 to 48 inches, in 3-inch increments), several depths, and a limited range of materials. Semi-custom, the next category up in cost and quality, gives you more options in terms of door styles, finishes, accessories, and trim.

The most expensive type of manufactured cabinets are custom-made upon order and built to the designer's exact specifications, from size and style to material and finish.

↑ **A DOUBLE-SINK VANITY** can double up on storage, too, with dedicated cabinets under each sink and shared drawers in the center. The furniture styling and marble top blend old-fashioned form with modern function.

REPURPOSING A VANITY

Few vanity styles look more at home in a traditional bathroom than a dresser profile, reminiscent of the washbasin look that was common before indoor plumbing. To get one for a bath today, you can choose from the many furniture-style vanities available, starting at around $500. Or, if you're handy (or know someone who is), you can easily convert an old dresser—or a modern one if that's more your style—into a sink cabinet. The conversion works best if the chest has doors and as few drawers as possible, to better accommodate the pipes. Then it's a fairly easy job to add an above-mount sink or, for an undermount sink, replace the top with stone or solid surfacing and cut an opening in the back to connect the plumbing. To complete the picture, swap out drawer pulls and door hinges for ones that match the other finishes in the room.

styles

Whether you have a lot of space or just a little, there's a vanity that fits

→ **A WALL-MOUNTED VANITY** adds style to a contemporary bath. This one comes with everything—under-sink storage drawers, open display shelves, even a medicine cabinet with lighted makeup mirror. All you have to do is add the sink and faucet. Most wall-hung systems are modular, with optional add-ons that you can tailor to your storage needs and the size of your space.

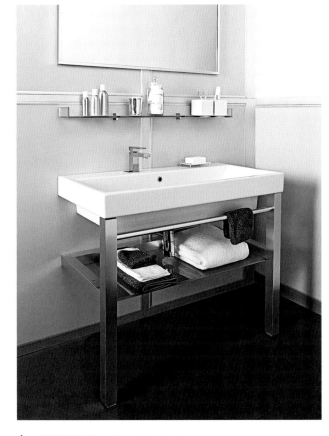

↑ **A CONSOLE** looks neat and clean but suffers from a lack of storage space. To remedy that shortcoming, many consoles come with shelving below and extra towel bars on the front or sides. This one has an above-the-sink shelf, too, to compensate for the limited deck space.

↑ **A FURNITURE-STYLE VANITY** is an easy way to give a small bath an instant period look. This powder-room-size model is 30 inches wide, with the fluted legs and turned feet of French Empire–style furnishings. The open cabinet below is big enough to hold a supply of guest soaps and towels.

>MEDICINE CABINETS

THE FIRST THING YOU SEE in the morning ought to look good, even if you don't. From classic to contemporary, above-the-sink cabinets provide a place to primp and space to stow toiletries. Recessed cabinets, which fit between studs and sit flush with the wall surface, save the most space, but surface-mounted cabinets are easier to install and have a more traditional look. Splitting the difference is a semirecessed style, which offers greater cabinet depth because part of it remains outside the wall. The standard height for the top of the cabinet box (not the frame) is 72 inches off the floor; you want to be able to see your face and some of your body in the mirror while still leaving room to place items on the sink below.

↓SURFACE-MOUNTED cabinets still look much the same as they did around the turn of the 20th century, when the bathroom as we know it today began to take shape.

↑RECESSED CABINETS come in a wide variety of styles, shapes, and sizes. They can be framed, like this one, or frameless, with a flat or bevel-edged mirror—a look well-suited to Art Deco–style baths.

easy upgrade

With these multitasking cabinets, simple storage is just the beginning

←REFRIGERATED A cabinet with a refrigerated compartment is just the thing for delicate cosmetics or temperature-sensitive meds. It's not cheap, but could be worth the expense if it saves you a trip to the downstairs fridge first thing in the morning.

→LIGHTED Where wall space is limited, a cabinet equipped with lights gives you storage and illumination in one neat package. This one, with cherry-stained wood, molding details, and satin-nickel fixtures, is styled for a traditional bath.

→ELECTRIFIED Never worry about a dead battery in your portable toothbrush or shaver if you've got a power strip hidden inside the medicine cabinet. In addition to convenience, a hardwired cabinet also keeps cords away from water and out of sight.

↑EXTRA DEEP Is your powder room so small that there's no place to store TP? You could stick a fuzzy cover on the extra roll and keep it in plain sight, but a deep medicine cabinet with two rounded cubbies just for that purpose looks much tidier.

>NOOKS + NICHES

THE STUD BAYS that lie empty behind drywall can yield ample stowaway space in even the tiniest bath. In the photo at right, a narrow sliver of wall between the bathtub and the towel rack houses a floor-to-ceiling built-in with a combination of open and concealed storage—shelves on top for easy access to everyday items and a cabinet below for unsightlies such as toilet paper.

If you plan to build recessed shelves in your bath, note that the standard width between studs is 14½ inches and the depth is 4 inches (if the wall is covered with ½-inch drywall). For anything deeper, you'll have to steal space from whatever is on the other side of the wall—in this case, the chase around an HVAC duct. Take care to locate plumbing pipes first to avoid running into obstacles when you open up the wall.

A tip: If you're annexing space from an adjoining room, don't just finish the back of the bumpout with drywall. Add wall-mount shelving; it's an attractive and functional disguise for the new construction.

↑**ONE STUD BAY** is all you need for powerhouse storage, as in this floor-to-ceiling cabinet that takes advantage of otherwise unoccupied wall space.

←ODD SPACES, like the dead zone under a roof slope, are perfect spots to build in shelving. Open shelves, like these made of red oak plywood trimmed with red oak nosing, maximize storage with minimal effort and expense.

↑A SHOWER NICHE neatly corrals bath necessities as it adds design possibilities. Line it with contrasting tile, add a marble bottom ledge, or frame it with a decorative border. The look is cleaner and more classic than wire baskets— and soap can't slip through.

→WALL NICHES are practical as well as decorative, holding towels or items for display. This deep, mirror-backed recess in an attic takes advantage of open space on the other side.

↑UNDER THE WINDOW is an ideal spot for a vanity shelf because it takes advantage of natural light for putting on makeup. Add a drawer below to store cosmetics.

>BUILT-INS

THE ULTIMATE IN custom bathroom organizing, built-ins keep essentials close by and clutter out of sight. They're also a surefire way to add character, style, and value to your home. You can use built-ins to highlight architectural details, make small spaces feel larger, or give big spaces a unified look.

The major benefit of built-ins is that you can take advantage of every inch of space, up to the ceiling and down to the floor. Even the most cramped bath has square footage with untapped potential, where you can build in cubbies, cupboards, and shelving units.

You're also not limited to available styles, colors, or materials when you work directly with a cabinetmaker. As a result, of course, there's almost no limit on what you can spend. But in a relatively small space like a bathroom, you don't need a big price tag to get a big return, in terms of style as well as storage.

A WALL-TO-WALL VANITY packs in storage with a seamless appearance. Finished along the top with crown molding that ends below the barrel-vaulted ceiling, it appears to be a single piece. Curved feet as well as flush inset drawers and doors add to the furniture look, while glass knobs and nickel fixtures give it Old World appeal.

←A 7-FOOT-HIGH ARMOIRE stands at one end of a built-in walnut tub surround. In addition to providing ample storage for the bath, it also functions as a privacy screen and room divider between the bathtub and the adjacent bedroom.

↓A DIVIDING WALL between two adjacent bathrooms contains a double-sided linen closet, which is accessible from either bath. The floor-to-ceiling unit also has cabinets and drawers that serve each space individually.

↑A BUILT-IN UNDER THE EAVES adds storage (a necessity with a pedestal sink) and keeps floor space open in a small attic bath. The low cabinet provides an additional surface and complements the cozy sloped ceiling.

→**A SUITE OF BUILT-INS** gives a master bath a dressing-room feel. His-and-hers vanities resemble chests of drawers, with mirrors hung above them and a hutch for bath supplies in between. Varying the heights helps give the pieces the look of freestanding furniture. The back of the open center section is lined with beadboard, for a casual look meant to evoke a New England seaside cottage.

↑**ENCLOSED DRAWERS** slip into a crawl space and turn underutilized square footage into a storage bonanza. Not all built-ins have to be crafted from scratch: These are prefab drawer units with medium-density fiberboard interiors. A skylight helps illuminate the contents and relieves the low ceiling.

←**GLASS-FRONTED CUPBOARDS** lighten the look of a floor-to-ceiling built-in while adding old-house character. If you're worried about keeping the contents looking neat, use woven baskets or other containers to hide clutter.

STORE EVEN MORE

You don't need a full-on bath remodel to increase storage and improve organization. There are plenty of easy and affordable ways to make the hardest-working room in the house work a little harder.

←ADD AN EXTRA CABINET. Recess an additional cabinet into the wall to augment what you've got over the sink. One made of wood or metal can tuck behind the door so that it's largely out of sight. At 6 feet tall and 8 inches deep, this semirecessed cabinet is big enough to organize the whole family, and adds a full-length mirror and electrical outlets besides.

→SQUEEZE IN A FREESTANDING PIECE. If there's room, slide in a salvaged footlocker or metal doctor's cabinet; you'll gain character as well as order. Narrow, new freestanding units do the trick equally well. This vintage-inspired tower is actually three separate pieces—a base unit, drawers, and glass-front cabinet—that can be configured however your space allows. To get the most from a freestanding piece, think first about how you're going to use it, so that it doesn't become another place to store junk.

←ORGANIZE THE INTERIOR. The functionality of existing cabinets can be improved with the addition of kitchen cabinet–style drawer dividers, slide-out shelves, and wire bins screwed to the inside of the doors.

→SEPARATE YOUR STUFF. To make sharing a bath easier, give each family member a dorm-style tote to corral personal supplies. That way everyone can keep track of their favorite items.

>CREDITS

p. 1: Photographs: (left to right) Jürgen Frank; Aimee Herring; Matthew Benson.

p. 2: Photographs: (left to right) Megan Chaffin; Grant Delin; Thibault Jeanson.

p. 3: Photographs: (left to right) Nathan Kirkman; Ray Kachatorian; Keller & Keller.

p. 7: Photograph: Julian Wass.

pp. 8–11: Photographs: Tria Giovan. Design: Erika Doering, Erika Doering Design. Illustration: Ian Worpole.

pp. 12–15: Photographs: Andrew Bordwin. Design: Robin Zahn, Robin Prince Zahn Architecture. Illustration: Ian Worpole.

pp. 17–19: Photographs: Alise O'Brien. Design: Kristin Collins Moomey, HKW Architects; Marcus Moomey, KAI Design & Build. Illustration: Ian Worpole.

pp. 21–22: Photographs: Mert Carpenter. Design: Esin Karliova and Remodel West.

p. 23: Photographs: John Gruen. Design: Thomas W. Hemmerick, architect. Illustration: Cynthia Ng.

p. 25: Photograph: Alex Hayden.

pp. 26–29: Photographs: Deborah Whitlaw Llewellyn. Design: Michael O'Keefe, architect; Kate Bartlett, designer, Home Rebuilders. Illustration: Ian Worpole.

pp. 31–33: Photographs: Erik Johnson. Design: George Myers, GTM Architects. Illustration: Ian Worpole.

pp. 35–37: Photographs: Keller & Keller. Design: Charlie Allen Restorations Inc., design/build contractor. Illustration: Ian Worpole.

pp. 39–41: Photographs: Alan Shortall. Design: Silent Rivers LC, design/build contractor. Illustration: Ian Worpole.

pp. 42–45: Photographs: Michael Luppino. Design: Jay Haverson, Haverson Architecture and Design PC. Illustration: Ian Worpole.

pp. 47–49: Photographs: Nathan Kirkman. Design: Karen Walker, KW Custom Design. Illustration: Cynthia Ng.

p. 51: Photograph: Eric Piasecki. Design: Steven Lecher, Lecher Development LLC.

p. 52: Photographs: (left) Linda Oyama Bryan; (right) Mark Samu. Design: (left) Dave Heigl, CabinetWerks Design Studio.

p. 53: Photographs: (top) Mark Lohman; (bottom) Jürgen Frank. Design: (top) Nick Berman Design; (bottom) Rick and Elizabeth O'Leary.

p. 54: Photograph: Linda Oyama Bryan. Design: Dave Heigl, CabinetWerks Design Studio.

p. 55: Photographs: (left) Jim Franco; (right) David Prince. Design: (left) Jay Haverson, Haverson Architecture and Design PC.

p. 57: Photograph: Grant Delin.

pp. 58–61: Photographs: Nathan Kirkman. Design: Chip Hackley, Hackley & Associates Architects. Illustration: Ian Worpole.

pp. 63–65: Photographs: Wendell T. Webber. Design: AnnMarie McCarthy and Mark LePage, McCarthy LePage Architects PC. Illustration: Cynthia Ng.

pp. 67–69: Photographs: Casey Sills. Design: Christine Julian, Julian Kitchen Design. Illustration: Ian Worpole.

pp. 70–73: Photographs: Wendell T. Webber. Design: Carol Kurth, Carol Kurth Architects PC. Illustration: Ian Worpole.

pp. 72: Photograph: (left) Michael Lewis.

p. 75: Photograph: Deborah Whitlaw Llewellyn. Design: Todd Pritchett, Todd Pritchett Design Studio.

p. 76: Photographs: (left) Stephen Karlisch; (right) Timothy Bell. Design: (left) Hollis Driskell, Hed Designs.

p. 77: Photograph: David Peterson. Design: Barbara Chambers, Chambers & Chambers Architecture and Interior Design.

p. 78: Photographs: (top left) Matthew Benson; (top right) Paul Whicheloe; (bottom) Matthew Millman. Design: (top right) Larry Mufson, The Mufson Partnership; (bottom) Amy Hall McNamara, Gordon Hall & Associates.

p. 79: Photograph: Josh Gibson.

p. 81: Photograph: Tria Giovan.

pp. 83–85: Photographs: Michael Jensen. Design: David Root, David Root Design. Illustration: Ian Worpole.

pp. 86–89: Photographs: Megan Chaffin. Design: David Roberts, David Roberts Architects Ltd. Illustration: Ian Worpole.

pp. 90–93: Photographs: Tria Giovan. Design: Barry H. Light, architect. Illustration: Ian Worpole.

p. 95: Photograph: Roger Davies.

pp. 97–99: Photographs: Evan Sklar. Contractor: Patrick McCormack, East Coast Interior Construction. Illustration: Ian Worpole.

pp. 100–101: Photographs: Megan Chaffin. Illustration: Ian Worpole.

p. 102: Photographs: (left) Eric Roth; (right) John Coolidge.

P. 103: Photograph: Stephen Karlisch.

p. 104: Photographs: (left) Laurey W. Glenn; (right) Lisa Romerein.

p. 105: Photograph: Lisa Romerein.

p. 106: Photographs: (top) Shelley Metcalf; (bottom) Deborah Whitlaw Llewellyn.

p. 107: Photographs: (left) Thomas J. Story; (right) Josh Gibson.

>INDEX